GIVE THE DRUMMER SOME

BY

BILL PASSMORE

"I LEARNED TO PLAY GUITAR TO GET THE GIRLS."

AC-DC

DEDICATION

To God, the creator of the universe.

To my wife, Chris, who has backed all my crazy ideas.

To Megan, my youngest daughter, for her help and support.

To Jesse, my youngest son, for his artistic contributions.

Especially to Helen Mullins, helping to put my thoughts into reality.

Give The Drummer Some
The autobiographic account of one man's pursuit of a career in music from the beginning of Rock & Roll in the 1950's through the explosive 1980's and into the 21st century.

© Copyright 2016 Bill Passmore

Author and Publisher, Bill Passmore
272 County Rd 587, Englewood, Tennessee 37329, 423-829-4831

Edited by Megan Pendergrass, Helen Mullins, and Ginger Malloy

All photographs property of Bill Passmore
Illustrations by Jesse Passmore

Cover and book design by Helen Mullins, HM Graphics, LLC, Etowah, Tennessee

ISBN # 9781792830518

Printed in the U.S.A. HM Graphics, LLC, PO Box 398, Etowah, TN 37331, 423-263-7548

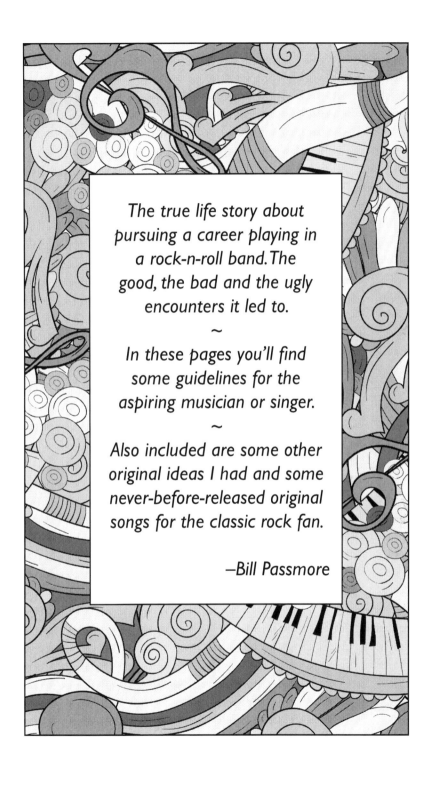

The true life story about pursuing a career playing in a rock-n-roll band. The good, the bad and the ugly encounters it led to.

~

In these pages you'll find some guidelines for the aspiring musician or singer.

~

Also included are some other original ideas I had and some never-before-released original songs for the classic rock fan.

—Bill Passmore

CHAPTER ONE
the beginning

Have you ever thought about writing your life story, or any story for that matter? I'm at that point in my life where I'm looking back at it all trying to decide if anyone is interested in reading about it. Oh, I've had a couple of friends tell me I should tell my personal stories. After all, I have done things and been places that most people never experience.

Ok, I think I'll travel down that road...

~

I turned 21 in Atlanta, Georgia, and stayed on the road most of my life playing music. All kinds of music. I had to if I wanted to survive.

Becoming a "star" in the music industry can be extremely difficult. It will chew you up and puke you out. I came close, but close will haunt you. It takes money, talent, the right place, and lots and lots of luck to make it in the music industry.

But, now that I think about it, I probably wouldn't be alive today if I had made the big time. We all know what happens sometimes, when a poor boy or anyone for that matter makes good in music.

We have lost many a good one to drugs and alcohol. That lifestyle will turn you inside out if you let it. I'm still here though, so let me take you back.

~

The trends that swept the world during the fifties, sixties, and seventies were definitely commiserate with that old saying – drugs, sex, and rock & roll! It's true and I lived and survived it.

I'm planning a fifties rock music reunion with the surviving members of my first band, "The Spades." It was the first organized rock group in the small town of Athens, Tennessee. And, that reunion will be over with by the time you are reading this book.

I'm looking forward to seeing everyone again. Its been twenty years since I've seen most of them and me at the young age of 73. Three of our band members have passed — Dennis Punkin Ballew (guitar), Steve Hambaugh (vocals), and Jerry Bradford (vocals). I miss them.

Some are still around though, there is Pete Hambaugh (bass), Bernie Wade (keyboards), Adrian Charles (sax), Steve Sitzlar (vocals), and Sara Lee (vocals). When Sara was only a child of fourteen I asked her, "Your name is Lee, could you sing like Brenda Lee?" "I don't know, maybe," she said. With that she became a Spade. Everyone loved her. She was and still is so cute.

Adrian went on to play saxophone with the "Bill Black Combo." Bill was Elvis' bass player when "The King" became the heart throb of the world. Punkin played with Bertie Higgins (*Key Largo* was Bertie's hit song) and also with Glen Campbell in Las Vegas.

I'm getting ahead of myself. You know I never learned to dance. I was always sitting behind a set of drums playing for the dancers.

Did I say, "Let me take you back?" Well, I started out in a small house next to Mouse Creek in McMinn County, Tennessee — which I don't remember. I came into this world on January 26, 1942. When I was older my dad took mom, my siblings and me back to that creek to swim. Man was that water cold.

The house was torn down before I was old enough to remember it. I was the second of five children. My mom (Lois) had a small child (my sister June) when she met Carmel Passmore (my dad). They then hatched me. Mom always told me she found me under a stump, which I believed for years. A year after I came along, my brother Danny was born, then little sister Kaye, and the last was my youngest brother David. We are all about five years apart except Danny. I got a 'whuppin' for nearly biting off Danny's toe one time — because I was jealous of the attention he was receiving from my parents.

When Danny was a year old, pneumonia and measles took his life. The doctors at our small hospital tried everything, but penicillin hadn't been discovered yet, which probably could have saved him. Sulfa drug was the strongest thing out at that time.

I was two years old, but I can remember my mom screaming. One of my relatives took me home. It was very traumatic, and I can remember that far back in my young life.

He was buried with a little lamb on his head stone. It's still there, but quite a bit worn. I've often wondered what it would have been like to grow up with a brother almost my age? Would he have been a musician, too?

This brings me to my younger sister. That girl would follow my friends and me everywhere. We hated that with a passion. I got more whippings because of her. I love little sis now, though.

We had a willow tree in our yard and mom would always get a good long branch from it and pop me on my back like a whip... OUCH!

Being poor, dad only made fifty dollars a week as custodian of the college in Athens. Mom would work part time at a hosiery mill and make extra money for school clothes and holidays.

The first pair of Levi jeans I owned was payed for by me carrying two newspapers before and after school. Mom bought everything from Sears and Roebuck catalogs. She sure could stretch a dollar – and I sure didn't take after her.

We always had a garden and chickens, although we lived in town. On Sundays dad would sling a chickens' head off by it's neck. We would clean it and mom would fix it for dinner. Back then we called it breakfast, dinner, and supper — today people refer to the mid day meal as lunch, and dinner is in the evening.

One day I decided to sling a chicken for dinner. I slung that bird around and around till it's neck was stretched six or seven inches long. That thang ran "crazy" with it's head hanging down at it's side. Freaked me out! Dad finally caught it and chopped it's head off. I lost my taste for chicken that day, so I never tried that again.

Not having a bathroom in the house, we used the outhouse or "johnny" (as we called it) outside. Man, was it cold in the winter and full of wasps in the summer. I got stung so much, I guess that's why I'm allergic to bees now. That Sears catalog really paid off then — you could sit and read or wipe with it.

9

It was so nice when dad and grandpa built a small bathroom inside the house. It had a toilet and bath tub. Now that's what up town funk means!

I did come close to getting electrocuted standing in that tub of water. We had a radio sitting on top of the small hot water heater. The plastic tuning knobs had long fallen off and only the metal was sticking out. I reached to change the station and it knocked me to my knees. All I know is it wasn't my time to go.

Chapter Two
a budding Musician

When Elvis came on the scene I started dreaming of becoming a musician — although my first desire was to be a jet fighter pilot. A motorcycle accident changed my life forever. A head on collision with my motor bike and a car ended the dream of being a pilot. It crushed my ankle and I couldn't pass the Air Force physical. The driver of the car was drinking, so he ran. That was my first encounter with an impaired driver.

Bill Haley and The Comets, along with Little Richard, had something to do with my decision, too. Mom decided I should take piano lessons, seeing that I was interested in music. She bought an old up-right piano and we found a good teacher.

Let me tell you something, those piano recitals were the most nerve racking things I believe I've ever had to do. I was a bashful kid and I would almost faint if I had to stand in front of the class at school.

One thing that would help me when it was recital time was to choose a "boogie woogie" type song to play. It made me more relaxed when the audience started tapping their feet, which I guess led me to playing rock & roll.

I never was all that good on the piano, but the recital audience always liked my song choices, that up-tempo style of music. If you want to be a musician, I recommend taking piano lessons because it teaches you music chords and tempo. I learned to read music which has paid off in my career, although I still play a lot by 'ear,' too.

I switched to drums, which came natural for me. I never had a lesson. It just felt comfortable — I just started "beating" on that drum. Bless my momma's heart! Later, I did learn to read drum charts which is completely different from piano or guitar.

Playing drums probably came from my dad, who could play a set of spoons as good as I have ever heard. Up and down his arms, and on his head he would go, and I mean GO! Man, he sure could put on a show.

There was a guy, on the country television show "Hee Haw," that played spoons, but my father could blow him away, and I'm not saying that just because he was my dad. I've been in this business long enough to know talent when I hear or see it. My dad and his buddies would jam together at our house now and then. They played the old country and western classics — such as Jimmie Rodgers and Hank Williams of the forties and early fifties.

My uncle Homer on my mom's side of the family would drop by and play piano at my grandmother's house which was next door to us. He played and sang the old standards and jazz songs, like *Star Dust* and *Moon Glow*. His main instrument was dog-house bass [a *dog-house bass is the big bass you play standing up. It has a leg and stands about five feet tall. All jazz bands and orchestras use these]*, and he was a lead singer in a jazz band. He has since passed on, but I can still hear him singing *Misty*. Having musicians on both sides of family, it was just a matter of time until I organized a band.

CHAPTER THREE
the Adventures of Zorro

As a young teenager my best friend Bob Jarvis and I were very mischievous. We grew up a block apart and became inseparable. Bob was the king of practical jokes who loved to play pranks on anybody he could, especially me. I'm sure he holds the record for paddle spankings in grammar school. Oh yeah, I got a few of those paddlings, too.

If I got a paddling at school, I knew when I got home my dad would have his belt ready. Even so, it taught me what kids are missing today — RESPECT! I loved my family and they loved one another. We were poor, but rich in a close family relationship. I wouldn't change it for anything.

Mom loved to make quilts, so all our beds had her homemade handy work. My bedroom was the last room in our 'straight line style' house. Mom kept my door closed in the winter so our coal burning heater could warm the rest of the house.

When it came time for bed, Mom would open my bedroom door and it would be freezing in there. When I crawled into that 'refrigerator,' I was under five quilts. It felt like ice, and for fifteen minutes or so, I would stay on my hands and knees until it warmed up enough to roll onto my side. When I got comfortable I slept like a bear that was in hibernation. To this day, I need to have my bedroom ice cold to sleep, and I freeze my wife Chris to no ends.

Somehow, with Mom's money skills, we were one of the first in our neighborhood to get a television. Reception was terrible and of course it was black and white. Bob and I got into shows such as the Lone Ranger, Black Hawk, and especially Zorro, our favorite. We came up with the idea to create a Zorro mystery character in our neighborhood. We both were fast runners, but I was recovering from that motorbike ankle injury and was still wearing a cast on my foot. Bob was Zorro, and brother did he take the part to heart and live it.

A lot of the guys around town had mopeds and scooters. One evening 'Zorro' made his appearance in a passage through a wooded area at the north part of our neighborhood. A friend, Dennis, came cruising down the trail on his moped, and out from behind a bush the masked figure shot out chasing him.

Zorro fired a warning BB pellet and ran beside him through the woods. Dennis was freaking out. He turned on the gas down to a hangout where all the bikers and cute girls were. Shaking, he excitedly told everyone about this dude dressed in black that could run as fast as his bike. Said he got shot at with a pellet gun. So, the mystery adventure was officially ON!

Talk of this spread all through the school, and every evening kids were looking to see Zorro. Sometimes he would show up unexpectedly anywhere, and usually someone would get stung with a pellet.

No one could catch him because he could just disappear. He was extremely elusive. Although I knew who Zorro was, the mystery was so much fun for everyone, that I just played along. I even got popped a time or two with flying pellets. Thank goodness no one got hurt.

The whole town was 'a buzz.' I think back on those times and realize that was some of the most exciting, fun shenanigans of my life. To this day, not too many people knew my best friend was Zorro.

I turned sixteen years old in the hospital with my ankle injury. I still have a screw through the bone, but lately it's been giving me some discomfort. I probably will have to get it out one day. Using that foot on the bass drum all those years kept it limber and normal.

Chapter Four

then Along came The Spades

Around this time (about 1958) I became interested in street rods. I bought a 1936 five-window Ford Coupe. It was powered by a 48 Mercury flat head V8 engine with a stick shift tranny.

It was my first car, but needed some work and a new paint job. I sold it and found a 1934 five-window Ford Coupe that had been customized. Man, what a killer looking street rod that car was! It was pink with a continental kit and purple seats, powered by a 57 Chevy V8 with straight shift gears. I got a lot of dates with that car!

Zorro was still around at that time, but now I was in a car, and I let the girls pile in to go looking for the 'mask.' That was nice and worth writing home about.

This lasted for about two years, boy what fun! It was the era of drive-in restaurants. Some of the best looking girls worked as car hops at these establishments.

Drag racing took place around these packed hot spots with rock and roll music blaring from 45 records in juke boxes.

I began playing drums, so with Bernie on the piano we put together a rock band. We were the first organized group who played that kind of music in Athens. As I explained earlier, we became 'The Spades.' We got that name from sitting around playing cards.

We tried different musicians, and our first lead singer was a black guy named Gene Woods. He sang songs such as *Hey Little Girl In The High School Sweater* by Dee Clark. Later, down the road, I played music with Dee Clark in Savannah, Georgia. At the time, Dee wanted our band to go on the road with him, but we had other plans and turned him down. He was a super good singer and a nice guy.

The Spades started playing assembly programs at our high school in McMinn County. We weren't that good in the beginning, but our classmates loved it. All I had at that time was an old marching snare drum. I did make a lot of racket with that 'thang' though!

We then, started performing at local skating rinks and drive-in restaurants on flat bed farm trailers. Our band grew to a ten piece group and became 'the band' around East Tennessee. Actually, we didn't have much competition.

A funny note I have to throw in — we bought an old up-right piano for Bernie to play on and moved it with a u-haul trailer. Electric pianos hadn't been out long, and we didn't have the money for one. Do you have any idea how much that old piano weighed? It was brutal moving it. It took about five or six guys to slide it, let alone pick it up. Now that's a love of music!

During this time a lot of kids fell in or out of love to the music of The Spades. I didn't realize it then, but what wonderful memories those were. I sort of did the love thing myself, a time or two, too.

We played a lot of black establishments which was a new thing back then. Music crosses all races and is color blind. We were always well received and made a lot of friends, many of which I still have today.

One of my favorite places was this huge skating rink and dance hall in Cleveland, Tennessee. The owner was James Mathews, but everyone just called him 'Saint James at the House of Happy Feet.' We would pull in around five hundred people on a Saturday night. Saint James made the best pork chop sandwiches around. We would let the rhythm and blues fly.

Gene decided to leave the group. He moved to California and became a gospel singer. We replaced him with a kid named Jerry Bradford — a white boy that could sing like Little Richard and Ray Charles. Sadly, Jerry passed away not too long ago. He fell through a roof on his job and was never physically well again.

Sara Lee (her maiden name) could sing like Brenda Lee, but also could perform rhythm and blues. One selection we did was the hit *Jim Dandy*, a great song to play.

When *What'd I Say* by Ray Charles came out, it was a natural for Bernie. He really did a good job on that one. By then we had an electric piano like Ray Charles. Jerry did Little Richard and Steve Sitzlar had Fats Domino down to a 'T.' I mostly sang backup then.

Our harmonies were similar to the Beach Boys and the Drifters. One fun song that I liked to perform was *At The Hop*. Elvis, Jerry Lee Lewis, and Carl Perkins were also on our play list.

We picked up a gig at the National Guard Armory in Cleveland, Tennessee every Saturday night. We would pull in over a thousand kids and young adults from as far away as Atlanta, Georgia. There was no age limit because alcohol wasn't sold. I've never seen so many good looking girls in my life. Oh, we thought we were hot!

Steve Hambaugh, our Bass player Pete's younger brother, was gifted with good looks, and was one of the more popular members of the band. Steve left the group when he was selected to be a cheerleader for the 'Big Orange' at the University of Tennessee at Knoxville. He was killed in a car wreck shortly after that — a shame at such an early age. I think of him often.

CHAPTER FIVE
Hot Rods and Music

Around this time I traded hot rods again. I swapped my 1934 Coupe for a 1932 five-window Ford Coupe. It was channeled low to the ground and was powered by a '55 Caddie V8 with a four banger carburetor. That machine would flat out scream!

I got into drag racing on quarter mile race tracks. A good friend, Darrell McMann and I went to school together and lived close to each other. Darrell was a mechanic at his father's garage. We mixed pure alcohol with gas and took my rod to the Loudon, Tennessee drag strip. It had racing slicks on back and that machine would eat up some asphalt. My mother called it the running gears of destruction.

I was the only teenager in high school with a 'pure' street rod. I had my own parking spot and when I was running late for school the kids would hang out the windows, cheering me on to beat the last bell for class. That was some great memories to hold on to. If only I knew then what I know now!

One day someone, somehow sneaked a skunk into the school and turned it loose. Classmates were puking and scrambling for the exits. It took quite a while to rid the skunk and smell out of that place. I never knew who thought that prank up.

One of the band members' sister was my first real sweetheart. Her name was Billie Ruth, but we called her Bue. I think her brother Steve hung that on her.

We went everywhere in my coupe. She and I dated for awhile, until one day she told me her mother was moving to Clearwater, Florida and taking her with her. We both were heartbroken.

The next Christmas break, Darrell my mechanic buddy said, "Let's go see Bue and her mother." He was related to them — I believe a nephew. He owned a 1940 Ford sedan, so we decided to drive it.

I had never been to Florida, and I sure wanted to see my girlfriend, but there was a problem with that sedan. It used oil like crazy, so we had to take a trunk full of that stuff. We had to stop and fill the engine up every fifty miles. It took forever to get down there. Only two teenagers would attempt such a thing.

We spent a few days in Clearwater, and went to the beach swimming in very cold water that time of year. It was my first time to see the ocean, so I just had to go in.

Bue and I promised to stay in touch until we could be together again. Being that age it didn't pan out, and we eventually went our separate ways.

The trip back to Tennessee got crazy, because the brakes went out and we only had enough money for gas. We had to use the emergency brake to slow down and eventually stop. Were we glad to see that Tennessee line.

~

While in high school, [Yes, I know I'm jumping back a little here], hot rods, chopper motorcycles, duck-tail hair styles, and rock & roll were happening. 'Dirty' dancing became a young people craze. I thought parents were going to have a seizure. I'm sure you've heard the history of what people said about Elvis Presley!

I decided to start my own hot rod club, so I got some of my friends with the right type cars to join me. I drew up the 'Chinese Charlie logo' for the jackets that we had made in Kansas City, and we became "The Travelers." The logo was a Chinese man with a long pony tail standing in a chariot with his hand on a tall gear shift. A blazing V8 engine in front with the flames shooting out the headers, and spikes on the wheels. He also had a whip in the other hand.

We had a reunion a few years back and five of the original members were there. Some still had their original jackets and can still wear them. I've put on too much weight, and even if I did

ATHENS, TENNESSEE
Est. 1958

still have mine, I couldn't get into it. I was tall and skinny back in those days. I wonder whatever happened to my jacket?

The Travelers still meet every third Saturday of the month in Athens, Tennessee. When I left the club to play music, I lost touch with the old and new members of the club. A friend of mine said he saw a 1934 Ford similar to the one I had. He said he saw it on the Internet for sale at $85,000. If only I knew then! We all say that about a lot of things, right?

Chapter Six
on the Streets of New York

Our piano player in The Spades got a part time job at the local airport. A small airfield with quite a few planes. It can handle small jets now, and has the museum of the World War II fighter, the 'Swift.' One thing on my bucket list is to go up in the greatest fighter ever built — a P-51 Mustang. The fastest propeller plane ever. It could hang with those first German jets because of it's maneuverability.

The airport housed a lot of private and business planes, and had a Cessna four-seater plane to give flying lessons in.

Bernie and a couple of friends of mine started flying lessons. After forty hours you flew solo and earned your 'wings.' All three of them got their pilot's license.

We would take that 172 up and do all kinds of fun stuff, like power on and off stalls, dives, and real sharp turns. They let me fly in the co-pilots seat. All we had to do was replace the fuel. I'm not sure why I didn't pursue that life opportunity, probably because it was expensive.

My three buddies became major airline pilots and Bernie still trains young pilots in the middle east.

One day we got a wild hair — Bernie, Adrian, and a pilot friend Jacky, decided to rent a Piper Comanche plane. It was equipped with retractable landing gear, seats four, and flew around 180 knots.

We wanted to go to New York City and hear Joey Dee and the Starliters sing their hit song *Peppermint Twist* at the Peppermint Lounge on 45th Street. We landed at the La Guardia Airport, took a bus to Times Square, and did the Peppermint Lounge.

It turned out, Joey was away on tour, but we still enjoyed the entertainment. Hey, we were in the Big Apple — our first time. None of us were of age, but they let us in anyway.

Later that night we went back and slept on the plane. We didn't have much money, but it was fun and crazy.

I got to fly part of the way back, but hit some thunderstorms and spent the night in Roanoke, Virginia, again in the plane.

~

Later on in my musical journey, I played a lounge called the Wagon Wheel, just a few doors down from the Peppermint, and owned by the same company. I had a band at that time named the Big Brothers.

This group consisted of seven members, one a girl that I later married. Her name is Barbara, but she went by Bobbi Lynn. I had my first child, Michelle and my first born son Ian with Bobbi. I must admit, Ian has more musical talent than I ever had. I love to hear him sing *My Maria* by Brooks and Dunn.

We were booked for a month and shared the stage with an all girl band called the Baby Dolls. They were good, but played all rock. They played an hour, and we played an hour until four o'clock in the morning.

The Big Brothers was a unique conglomerate that performed rock, but specialized in rhythm & blues. We played tunes by Aretha Franklin, Wilson Pickett, James Brown, Righteous Brothers, etc. When we first started playing, the audience was mostly white with a good crowd. When we left, it was predominantly black because they came early and stayed late. The Wagon Wheel was packed out.

Word had spread, "You got to hear these white dudes that play James Browns' album, 'Live at The Apollo Theater.'" It wasn't long until black entertainers that finished at two in the morning, came to hear us or sit in with us.

New York City never shuts down — it runs on all cylinders twenty-four hours a day. I would have breakfast around eight o'clock in the morning and listen to rock bands. One band, in particular, was this Japanese group that sounded good, but looked strange singing in English.

King Curtis and his Orchestra was doing shows in town. He heard about us and showed one night at the 'Wheel,' up in a front row seat. King was a sax player that recorded on most rhythm &

blues songs recorded in the 50's and 60's. Groups like The Coasters who had hits, *Yakety Yak* and *Young Blood*.

Our sax player was a bundle of nerves with Mr. Curtis sitting there, although James didn't have to worry. He could flat blow a horn. King liked what he heard because he came back.

We got to meet James Brown and he autographed his new album, "James Brown to James White."

We saw him perform in New Jersey and we were the only white people there. He definitely was one of a kind and I loved his show.

I just watched the movie "Get On Up" produced by Mick Jagger. It is the life of James Brown. The movie brought back many memories.

The club owner at the 'Wheel' hung a nickname on us — he called us the "bible belt, blue eyed soul band."

Johnny Maestro, who had a hit with *16 Candles*, was playing the Peppermint Lounge and had a killer show. He and I had breakfast together many mornings. He was a quiet person with a pleasant personality. It's hard to believe he grew up on the streets, but he had the scars to prove it.

CHAPTER SEVEN
taking it to Atlanta

I guess you've noticed I'm writing this like I'm just telling my story to someone. It helps me to remember the music stories of years ago. I hope I can shed some light to anyone who is passionate about a musical career. Music has made me rich in travel and seeing a world of different people. I would have never gotten out of Tennessee if not for it.

I'm also staying away from most curse words, even thou people tell me that's what sells books, but I think not. I never said a curse word in front of my mom and dad — that I can remember. I had too much respect and love for them. Now I have cursed a bunch. Matter of fact, I did a lot of stupid things which I will address in a couple of these chapters.

~

I lost my father when he was only 46 years of age. He had a bad heart valve from scarlet fever and died having open heart surgery. His early death was the hardest thing I've ever gone through. When I saw my band, The Spades, carrying my dad at the funeral, I wanted to die myself.

I then lost my mother ten years later at the age of 57. She was never the same without my dad those last few years. It didn't get any easier when I lost her. Both my parents died from heart problems. I've gone through most of my life without my mother and father. I know I will see them again, though!

After that first New York trip, The Spades decided to get serious about music. We hired a booking agent, cut the band down to six members, changed our name to The Dolphins, and headed to Atlanta to seek our rock & roll fortune.

Bob, our booking agent, was an opera singer and a good one. He taught us some voice lessons and I highly recommend that any one who sings take voice lessons. He booked us in a very popular club downtown — "Leb's Pig Alley." It was under a nice family restaurant, but looked like an outside French cafe. The waitresses dressed in cute little French costumes and did a dance routine with the band every hour. The Spades also dressed in French costumes — berets and all. We played some Greek and French songs, but let the hammer down on rock & roll.

We were booked for two weeks, but stayed almost a year. We met quite a few 'stars' while performing there. I met Ronnie Milsap at the Playboy Club just a block from the Pig Alley. Ronnie did a Ray Charles show that was outstanding.

More names later but back to Ronnie. Before he became big in country music, Ron did blues and rock. He came to hear us on his off night and we got to know him pretty well. The Playboy Bunnies would drop by and dance. In regular clothes they looked, well, like normal girls. Its amazing what costumes can do.

One night an entourage came in escorting this beautiful woman. This 'ole country boy from Tennessee was looking at Jane Mansfield. She was beautiful! She was doing a show at one of the auditoriums and decided to come see us. She liked our band, especially the Little Richard songs.

We all got our picture taken with her and I still have mine somewhere in all the things I've collected over the years. Not long after that, she was killed in a car wreck. Jane was a real sweet person.

We always had lots of our friends from Athens come down and visit with us. Our little following had started growing.

One day we went to rehearsal and stopped upstairs to eat lunch. All of a sudden Bernie punched me and said, "Is that who I think it is?" Sure enough, sitting there was none other than Marty Robbins. Not being able to resist, Bernie went bopping up to him and said, "Ain't you Marty Robbins?" He smiled, said yes and told us he was doing a concert that night. One thing led to another and we introduced ourselves as the band downstairs in the 'Pig Alley' lounge. He was surprisingly cordial and asked if we were there to rehearse. When we said "Yeah," he asked if we would mind if he went down and hung out with us? We about jerked his arm off and heading downstairs.

We went to the stage and he picked up Punkin's guitar, and strummed a few chords. I still can't believe we started jamming with Marty Robbins. He played us some of his hits and showed Punkin the guitar licks Grady Martin played on his smash recording, *El Paso*. Marty said Grady would turn so no one could see his original guitar chops in the recording studio. That's a guitar player for you.

Marty Robbins had one of the most beautiful voices in the music industry. It was like a perfectly pitched instrument. He was more western than country, and there is a big difference – country music was more "hillbilly" and western was Texas swing like Bob Wills.

We all got his autograph and had a once in a lifetime afternoon. We didn't get a single practice song accomplished, but it was worth every moment because he had a bad heart and left this world way too early in life.

Chapter Eight

hitting the road to LA

One day in Atlanta we met a singer with a popular gospel group that was playing a convention at one of the many auditoriums in town. We introduced ourselves and chatted with the young man a while. He then told us something that caught me off guard. I was raised in church, basically children's Sunday school classes, when I was a kid. I always had that religious background, even thou I got out into the "world."

Anyway, the young man, which I can't remember his or the group's name said, "Do you know what we say in our little prayer on stage before we sing?" I was expecting something nice — wrong! He said they would huddle and say "Lord help us kick the other groups asses." Whoa, that really stuck in my brain. I thought Atlanta was an evil place, which is not so. It's just a big city and proves I was just a small town country boy.

Later, after I picked up some street smarts, I figured out Atlanta was a typical modern city, and I spent a lot of time there. Our booking agent, who we figured out was bi-sexual and married with children, wanted to take us to Los Angeles and make a go of it. He would book jobs along the way on our journey to California.

Our first booking was a gig in Pensacola, Florida at the Paradise Club on the beach. That was a fun gig. From there we went to Gulf Shores, Mississippi and stayed in this cheap motel for two weeks waiting for our agent to get our next job.

I never saw so many mosquitoes in my life. The wind was blowing out from the swamps, carrying those little varmints with it. You would run as fast as you could, but they still landed and covered your body. I never experienced anything like it. Even though they sprayed with their mosquito trucks, we didn't venture out unless it was absolutely necessary.

I did learn to crab fish on an ocean dock. We tied chicken parts on a string, lowered it into the water and those stupid crabs would hang on until you pulled them off. They sure were delicious when boiled — mm mm good.

We finally got a gig at a night spot called the Red Lion Club in Beaumont, Texas. After arriving there, we found out they had a house band and we were booked as the guest band.

Now, I had never met an albino person but there were two in the house band. The guitar player and a sax player. Of course they were brothers. This group was none other than Johnny Winters and the Beaumonts. Brother Edgar (on sax), was only seventeen at the time, as I was told. You talk about laying down some Texas blues, and Edgar had perfect pitch. You could play a chord behind his back and he could tell you exactly what it was. He was so talented and could play just about any instrument, even the dog-house bass. He left the guitar to his big brother John, or should I say the original 'Johnny B. Good.'

We became good friends with these guys and they liked the way we played rhythm & blues. The first week we swapped sets, but the second week we joined together both bands, two drummers and all. Man, what a horn section, because they had two horns and one was Edgar — Whoa!

One night the club brought in a big time blues artist, Sonny Boy Williams. He came in with just a case of harmonicas, one for every key. We backed him up, layin' down some back porch, low down blues.

Later on, the Beaumonts left Texas and blew Atlanta, Georgia away. They made the 'big time' together, then separated to go their own ways. Edgar teamed up with Rick Derringer and Dan Hartman who came up with such hits as, *Frankenstein, Rock and Roll Hoochie-Coo*, and *Free Ride*. Edgar was tabbed as the number one alto saxophonist by Playboy magazine for about ten or twelve years in a row. 'White Trash' was his first band. I used to call him every now and then. Johnny, rated one of the best blues guitar players, passed away not to long ago. B. B. King also recently passed away. Too many good ones are leaving this world.

After the Red Lion, our destination to Los Angeles evaporated, so we went back to Tennessee and eventually our band members went their separate ways. I wonder sometimes how far we would have gone had we made it to LA.

Chapter Nine
kickin' it Around in Georgia

I kicked around for awhile with different musicians, keeping the name The Dolphins. I hooked up with another booking agent in Atlanta, so Pete, Bob Shoemaker on guitar, and I got a gig in Savannah, Georgia at a place called the Bamboo Ranch, where we stayed on as the house band for a while.

One day we met a sax player who became one of my best friends, James Moody. He had a great sense of humor and was definitely an "upper." We really had some good times together and the four of us became a decent band.

About once a month, the club owner would book a name group and at times we had to back them musically. Some of the groups were the Platters, the Drifters, and Janis Joplins' band Big Brother & The Holding Company.

The Platters came in on a Saturday with a music director. He handed us music charts and we practiced for only two hours. It was some of the hardest songs I've ever tried to play. They did a lot of broadway music but we made it through the show that night.

The Drifters had their own band and their biggest request was always White Christmas, any time of the year.

The Holding Company played some of Janis' songs and the drummer did a solo, *[give the drummer some]* without sticks, just his hands. Um, I wonder why he didn't feel any pain?

Sam the Sham came one night and we played for him. Some of his hits were *Wooly Bully* and *Little Red Riding Hood*. It was fun — even thou Sam was a little weird.

One of our favorites was Dee Clark, as I mentioned earlier. We fell right into his routine and enjoyed playing for him.

~

30

Shortly after Barbara and I were married we moved to Chattanooga, Tennessee where we formed a new band called Bobbi and The Blenders. We took a job as the house band at a popular night spot called The Go Go Club. The place was huge and held hundreds of people.

Billy, the club owner, really liked our band and we became good friends. He was always doing crazy things to promote his club. Once he had an artist paint a giant boa constrictor snake completely around the room, glowing with black lights. The lighting systems were always being changed, and the place was always packed.

One day Billy bought a baby African lion that had been smuggled into the United States. The lion was only a few months old and he took that cub everywhere, especially to the club. Everyone loved him because he was so playful.

I went to Billy's house every chance I got to play with that lion. He liked to jump on you when you were sitting and bite on your head. At that age his paws were as big as my hand. Sadly one night, Billy had him chained on his outside deck and he tried jumping off, hanging himself. Discovering it the next morning, Billy's heart was broke — as was mine, we loved that lion cub.

Go Go Billy was a body builder and a competitive weight lifter in the southern part of America. He won quite a few contests in his division.

CHAPTER TEN
the Turkey Dolls and the Black Widow

I'm going to back up again, so I can tie in my story about one of the most adventurous, rebellious, and colorful people I have ever had the chance to know.

I want to tell you the story about one of the most handsome, muscular, and tough street fighting human beings that came out of this part of the country. I had the privilege of growing up around him, and his life twisted and turned like a broken road that led him to an almost super human life. He was known as the Black Widow!

I know the female spider is the dangerous one, but it will make sense when I'm through telling you about him.

This true story is about the life and times of a small town street gang called the Turkey Dolls, and it just so happens Bob and I grew up around these guys. We all came from poor families in the northern part of Athens, Tennessee.

Growing up in the Fifties era, as you probably know, it was the birth of rock & roll, leather jackets, pink shirts, blue suede shoes, street rods, and chopper motorcycles.

Drive-in restaurants were the place to be and drag racing usually went down at one of these establishments. Can you believe it was only a fifty dollar fine if you got caught and we hardly ever got caught. There were not many cops in those days, and it was hard to catch a fast hot rod on the back streets of town.

Sock hop dances (kicking your shoes off in the school gym), and softball games were popular. And, yes, "Daddy-O" was spoken then.

Back to the main character of this care-free part of my life — J. R . Dockins (or as he was known later, the Black Widow). He was born more muscular than most of us and possessed uncanny good looks. He had black hair and looked a lot like Elvis. Impersonating his moves and lip-sing songs, the girls would go ballistic. You could say J. R. was one of the first impersonators.

He was a rebel's rebel, and would steal anything that wasn't tied down. J. R. was the most fun seeking, mischievous kind of "outlaw" I ever ran across. What amazed me most was that the girls were crazy about this bad boy Robin Hood.

All the Turkey Dolls would look for a rumble and start fights, especially at football games with guys from rival high schools. Most carried switch blades knives and belts made of chains.

Another past time was boxing. Being about three years younger, and growing up in the same neighborhood, the members took Bob, my best friend and me under their "wings." They did pull some pretty wild practical jokes on us. Now that I think about it, that's saying a lot because Bob turned out to be the "king" of practical jokes.

Some of the guys in this wild bunch was Chick, Boosey, Pat, Jack, and of course J. R. In my opinion Chick was the best bare knuckles street fighter of the group.

One night the Spades played at the national guard armory, and another bunch of rowdies showed up from a neighboring town. Well, as luck would have it, the Turkey Dolls came rolling in. One thing led to another and sure enough, this big 'ole country boy starts mouthing off so Chick takes it up.

I saw what was fixing to happen so we took a break from the music and the two guys went out into the parking lot and the fight was on. It has to go down as one of the greatest fist fights I have ever witnessed, and I have seen and even been in quite a few.

They swapped licks quick as a rattlesnake, like game cocks, and it seemed like it went on for an hour. It came down to which was the toughest and had the most endurance. Finally, I could tell Chick was wearing him down. At the end, the big boy said "enough," I had witnessed one hell of a street fight and if I had that on film I could've make some big bucks selling it to a promoter. It was as good as any fight you could've seen on television or anywhere.

All the Turkeys and friends were cheering and slapping Chick on the back. He was the "champ" on that particular night.

Jack was probably the best pure boxer of the group, even though my friend Bob was in the mix. He was somewhere in the middle weight class, always fighting in local matches. At that time, Jack was undefeated.

A huge heavy weight boxer, older than Jack, was making a name for himself. The local boxing club came up with the idea of matching the two together in a professional meet. A good deal of money could be made because of their reputations.

Jack, who wasn't afraid of anything said "Let's go," so it was set up. That same national guard armory was selected to hold the event. A ring was built, advertising was taken care of, and tickets went on sale. A big deal for little 'ole Athens, Tennessee.

When the fight started that big boy looked like a giant next to Jack, but remember he is a "Turkey Doll." That big dude charged Jack like a bull swinging hay makers, but you can't hit someone like the comic book character, "The Flash." Every time he swung, Jack would move and counter punch — float like a butterfly, sting like a bee and this was before Cassius Clay (aka. Mohammad Ali).

Pretty soon Jack was hammering him so hard and fast that his face was beginning to swell. His eyes were taking a beating.

The fight went the distance, but Jack had hit him unmercifully like a gunslinger. Needless to say Jack won the fight.

I heard not too long ago that Jack had entered a tough man contest — he is three years older than me! I don't know whether he won or lost, but I guarantee that his opponent knew they were in a dog fight.

~

J. R. was all of these things I've wrote about, except he did it with a big grin on his face. He was wild as a wolf and cunning as a fox.

One night a car full of guys came cruising up from another neighboring town to one of the many drive-in restaurants. It would take about thirty minutes to get from Cleveland to Athens because of the two lane highway and having to go through traffic lights.

It just so happens J. R. was there that night. Always looking for fun, he spots the guys with the Bradley County tags. Stepping up to the car, he gives a challenge to anyone who would take him

34

on. No one in the car would get out, and I don't blame them. You would think four or five guys might gang up on him, but with the motorcycle boots and the leather jacket they could tell he was a bad ass.

So J. R. whips out his belt style chain and starts beating that car like a wild man. Damage to the hood and lights were inflicted on that poor car before they could get out of the parking lot, disappearing down the road and never to return. Just one of many crazy things he would do.

Mr. Dockins got himself a knock-around car to drive and one evening he pulls up to a small cafe downtown to get a burger. As soon as he parked the car, this guy he had a run-in with caught him with a knife all the way down his face, barely missing his eye. J. R. reacted by slamming the door into the man knocking him back. Quick as a wink, he was on him, wrestled the knife away and almost killed him with his fist. It was a good thing the hospital was only a block away when the cops got there.

The attacker survived but was hospitalized for a couple of weeks after being beaten so badly. J. R. claimed self defense, but had a deep scar on his face for the rest of his life. He was never bothered by that character again, and the Black Widow's reputation was growing.

My father Carmel, whom I named my youngest son after, was an avid boxing fan and wasn't bad himself. He bought me a set of boxing gloves for Christmas one year when I was around fourteen. Now, Bob and I got involved in boxing match at school and the with the YMCA league. I got fairly decent, but Bob took to boxing like a duck to water. He moved to Knoxville, Tennessee and trained under the well known coach Ace Miller. Big John Tate, who won the heavyweight championship of the world, was one of Ace's boxers.

Bob trained hard and worked his way up and got a shot at the state championship. He won the fight to become the golden gloves champ in his weight division and held it for two years.

All the weight division champs and the state champions went on exhibition tours to raise money for the Knoxville boxing club's facilities.

One night in Cherokee, North Carolina the audience was asked if anyone wanted to go a couple of rounds with Bob. It was supposed to be for fun. This Indian kid said he would. Not thinking much about it, he and the Indian squared off in the ring, something he had done many times on tour.

After a few sparring punches by each other, the Indian boy caught Bob off guard square in the nose, and that punch was the end of his boxing career. That kid hit him so hard Bob was out for a while. He was taken to see a doctor who told him it ruptured a sinus in his face close to the brain. It could be fatal if he was hit hard enough again. It devastated him because he loved boxing and wanted to make a run at it. I had sparred with him and I knew he would do good in the sport.

My opinion is the Indian was tougher than expected, but I think Bob was too confident and let his guard down. He later married, and he has two daughters and lives in Knoxville.

~

I told that side story to tell this. One day foolishly, I was talked into getting into the ring with my "buddy" J. R. Oh my head! He was much bigger and older than me. J. R. said, "Now Bill, I'll take it easy, we're just going to spar." Yeah, right! I should have known better because you couldn't trust a word he said. All my neighborhood friends were there, so what was I supposed to do?

I climbed in that ring, and sure enough he showed me no mercy, beating on me like a drum. I threw everything I had at him, but to no avail. I took a whuppin' that day. Afterwards I said to J. R., "I thought that we were just supposed to spar." J. R. just looked at me with that smirky grin.

Halloween was a real riot back in those days. The "Turkey Dolls" were at their most outrageous behavior and so were me and Bob — turning over outhouse toilets, farm wagons lifted upon barns, VW beetles picked up and put in places where the owners couldn't get them.

We would make human like dummies and push them on ropes out into on coming cars. Always, there would be a rumble or fight, and in costumes you couldn't tell who was who.

One Halloween we all got together with a big metal drum can and filled it with used motor oil. Hauling it to a steep road, we poured that barrel of oil all over the street and hid in the bushes to watch the fun.

Cars couldn't make it up and slid every which way. I can't believe no one wrecked. It was at a slow speed zone, so I guess that was why. The only car to make it up that hill was an old power glide automatic Chevy. It was a funny thing to watch. The driver got a standing ovation.

That bit of foolishness was used again one cold winter night with water and ice. A large water hose hooked in my mechanic friend's garage on top of a hill over-looking downtown Athens, created a solid sheet of ice. Man, did the traffic have a rough time maneuvering that hill with a solid sheet of ice on it. The police had to detour traffic around that hill until it warmed up.

As I have stated, in those days the city didn't have many policemen, so we got away with racing and stuff that you would be put in jail for now.

One of the Zorro things was to hide at dusk behind the ballpark outfield and shoot the players in the butt with his BB gun, making it hard to play a game. The ball players would run through the little wooded area trying to catch him, but never could. Zorro would disappear into the darkness of the night.

A lot of people thought the Zorro character was J. R. but eventually figured it had to be someone else. Even the Turkeys couldn't solve the mystery.

~

J. R. Dockins (aka: the Black Widow) met this girl and fell in love. She was a beauty, but eventually became the downfall of my 'ole buddy. J. R. was a man that never should have married. His womanizing after they were married was just too much for her to accept. They did have a child, a boy that looked just like his dad.

The Turkey Dolls liked to hear us play, especially since Roger, my first guitar player was a Turkey. Roger is still playing today, he can pick Walk Don't Run by the Ventures note for note. His guitar was the first Fender guitar I had ever heard in person.

You never knew what to expect from this guy. He was a drinker at an early age. One night he got so wasted while playing he crashed backwards over his amp. We dragged him to a chair and carried on. It was the next morning when he fully understood what had happened.

This guitar player created a sound used by the Turkey Dolls. They would do it to agitate people, and by shaping their hand like a claw, they would stick it in your face and screech like an owl or something. It was a unique thing that turned out to be feared by the people that knew of them. When they all would do it together it was eerie.

One of the rival gangs came out of the poorest places in Athens. A slum area that covered a lot of the west side of town called "Tin Can Holler." It got that name because years earlier people used it for a garbage dump, especially metal cans that food and most everything was sold in. You couldn't dig a hole without turning up old rusted tin cans.

A lot of people lived there in cardboard shanties or huts made from most anything. It was a huge homeless type town all it's own.

It was a rough part of town, but it was also a close knit family place. Fighting, incest and even murder went on in the holler. The locals were mean and ran in packs. Most guys were shaving in grammar school, and that was about as much schooling as they ever got.

The girls were as rough as the boys. I witnessed many fights with girls going toe to toe with the guys. You didn't want to date one of those girls.

I got into a fight with one of those holler boys the first day of my school in the first grade. He pushed me off the merry-go-round and we wound up in the principal's office. Most of those guys are good friends of mine today. A lot have passed on.

A book has been written by a lady that was from that holler — "Tragedy in Tin Can Holler," by Rozetta Mowery. A must read with a lot of history about the place.

~

J. R. was always getting into trouble and decided to move on to Chattanooga, Tennessee. Soon after he married his girlfriend, he realized the mistake he made. He was too much of a woman chaser to settle down.

A lot of his friends had moved on with their lives or had gotten killed. He landed a job with a workout gym and was the perfect specimen of a body builder which made hiring him a no-brainer. He worked on his physique and could have been the cover photo of a muscle magazine.

Billy, the owner of the Go Go Club worked out at the same popular gym as J. R. He and J. R. become close friends. They started competing against one another and J. R. joined Billy in weight lifting contests. Between the two of them it was a toss up who would come away the winner since they were both extremely strong.

Billy hired J. R. as a bouncer at the club which was right down his alley. He loved to fight so he took that job seriously, keeping the rowdies in line. One night he smashed a beer pitcher on a man's face. They had to call an ambulance. The meaner they were, the better J. R. liked it.

Being the house band at the Go Go Club for those couple of years was how J. R. and I rekindled our friendship. Playing music on the road after high school, I lost touch with all my old friends and family, but J. R. and I stayed in touch, like when we were younger growing up.

The club was segregated in those days and the NAACP wanted to hold a boycott on an up-coming night. J. R. and Billy were ready when they found out the exact night it was going down. They were up on the roof with rifles and confronted the leaders head on, so they quickly decided it wasn't worth messing with these two crazy guys. They loaded back up and left, never to return.

I think it wasn't a racist thing, but more of a situation because Billy was the kind of person you did not tell him what to do. It wasn't too long after that Little Richard did a concert in town and Billy invited him, his band, and crew to the Go Go after the concert. Man, did we have one crazy jam session. Little Richard put on a show like he always did.

Working at the gym J. R. would instruct quite a few of the local police officers of Chattanooga. He, with that charming personality, was invited to join the force.

Drawing by
Jesse Passmore

A street gang member turned cop was an exciting offer — whoa!
A new challenge and it would all be legal.

This is where the story of J. R. Dockins really takes on a most
unusual twist that sets him apart from any cop that you could ever
imagine. Right off the bat he wanted to be a motorcycle policeman.
They gave him a solid white Road King Harley, of course. It was a
beautiful bike trimmed in black and he kept it spit shined. Now heres
the wild part, on the windshield he had a large painting of a black
widow spider to go along with all the blue lights. He wore puffy leg
riding britches, a leather police coat, boots, and gloves all black. He
had a long white scarf around his neck to go with his white helmet

that had the black widow emblem on the front of it, and fitted with a tinted face shield. You couldn't tell who he was if you didn't know him. He carried a large hand gun on one side and a holstered pistol grip, double barreled, sawed off, twelve gauge shotgun on the other. I bet he had knives in his boot, too!

J. R. was a sharp dresser without a wrinkle anywhere. Man, what an ominous looking creature he was, and with that fighting spirit, that thirst for a challenge, he quickly became top cop in Chattanooga.

How he got away with the dress and work codes I'll never know? A sawed off shotgun, a black spider? Maybe it had something to do with him being cop of the month regularly, catching more law breakers than most.

He was popular with his comrades and his reputation spread like wild fire. The bad guys feared the thought of that name — The Black Widow!

He would chase you down if you were in a car or on foot with his bike. He could run you down and have you pinned in a heartbeat. You couldn't get away from him. He was an early version of "Robo Cop," and no one wanted to mess with that shotgun. He was so good at his job, I guess they had to bend the rules.

J. R. continued to bounce at the Go Go in his off time, so he knew my schedule and time I would be coming into the city limits of town. When he was on duty he would be waiting on us riding that motorcycle and would proceed to give us a police escort down the four lane street to the club. Here we went with blue lights flashing doing sixty and seventy miles an hour passing everything in sight.

What a trip that was, and I can still see that long white scarf flapping in the wind. We thought we were something being escorted. I guess you could say...knowing people in high places, or is that high people in places.

He was a terrible husband, being unfaithful to his spouse and all. Too many women wanted to see that Arnold Schwarzenegger body that he had and with a face that resembled Elvis Presley, he was hard to resist. His wife took it about as long as she could. They had a child so a divorce was something he really didn't want. He really cared for her in his own twisted way, and he didn't want anybody else to have her but they did eventually divorce.

It was hard for her to date because everyone knew J. R.'s reputation. Finally, this one guy started seeing her but J. R. knew everything that went on in her life.

One evening while her boyfriend was visiting, J. R. found out, so he went busting into her house and confronted him. After knocking him down, J. R. started beating the crap out of him. He was wearing his pistol which turned out to be a careless mistake.

J. R.'s ex-wife was afraid that J. R. was going to kill her boyfriend so she reached out and grabbed his gun in all the commotion of the fight. J. R. turned toward her and one shot from his pistol goes through his heart. He was so strong any normal man would have collapsed right there, but he ran out the door across the lawn towards his vehicle and then dropped to the ground. The once great street fighter turned cop was dead!

At that time I was playing for the Strategic Air Command in Goose Bay Labrador, Canada. This is a refueling air base for the B-52 bombers that fly non-stop around the Arctic Circle in our first line of defense.

My younger sister Kaye was with me on this trip, and she received a phone call from a friend back in the states. Turning to me with a strange look on her face said, "J. R. Dockins was killed last night." This wild and crazy person I grew up with was gone.

It's like you can remember where you were when John F. Kennedy was shot. I got this empty feeling in my stomach, and it made the second friend I had lost in that period of my life. I lost another great friend, Frank McNutt — he was killed in a motorcycle accident.

I thought about J. R.'s ex-wife and what she must have gone through. She probably saved her boyfriend's life, because J. R. would have probably beat him to death. So some food for thought, the female spider has the power to kill, right? Whom then was the Black Widow?

CHAPTER ELEVEN

rockin' it in with The Blenders

While me and The Blenders were still playing Chattanooga, Billy moved down the street into a new club called The Castaway, but while there he got charged and convicted of having a competitive club burned down. He was sent to prison, and I've never heard from him since.

We got booked into another celebrity club in Chattanooga and performed with the *Down In The Boondocks* singer, Billy Joe Royal.

We lived there for awhile when my son Ian was born. Not being a very good husband I was soon divorced, even thou I have tried to be a good father. I guess my children can decide that better than anyone.

During this time in Chattanooga I met Charlie McCoy and The Escorts. Charlie is from Florida but moved to Nashville to seek out a musical career. One day a studio producer asked him if he played drums, and being hungry he said, "Yeah," even though he had never played them before. Somehow, he faked it through the session — he was that naturally talented. His main instrument was harmonica, but he can play just about anything.

Charlie was on most of Elvis' recordings, usually on harp. He said Elvis would come into the RCA Studios, and really liked to pal around, tell jokes, and order food for everyone. It would be the next day before they would get down to recording. Charlie didn't mind. He would sleep on the carpet floor, and being booked as the leader of the session he made double. The musicians were paid by the hour.

The guitar player in Charlie's band was a very good song writer, Mac Gayden. He wrote a couple of hit songs, one that has been redone a bunch of times. His first was *She Shot A Hole In My Soul* and his big one, *Everlasting Love*. Bobbi and the Blenders recorded one Mac wrote called *Earthquake*. We used a song I wrote on the B-side.

Back in those days it was 45 vinyl records with a song on each side. Technology has changed all that and for the better. *Opportunity Street* was one of the first songs I had written and it was definitely a B-side kind of song. Hey, you have to start somewhere. I did write one way back then called *Ask Me No Questions* and Lynyrd Skynyrd came out with one that was named the same thing.

Charlie took us to a recording studio that he and his partner owned. It was named Cinderella Studios, located on the East side of Nashville. It was the first time I had ever been in a professional studio, even though it was small.

His partner was a guitar player and a very good recording engineer. His name was Wayne Moss, and he made a name for himself as "Barefoot Jerry." Charlie Daniels sang a song about him in his hit, *The South's Going To Do It Again*.

Charlie was very creative. He had an off brand organ in his studio, and he could make that thang sound like a section of violins. It sounded so good on *Everlasting Love* and *Motown Sound* songs, I do mean "thang," it was amazing.

After pitching *Earthquake* to some record labels, we were signed to Bell Records in New York. We started getting some air play on radio and one station Charlie wanted to get us on was the famous WLAC in Nashville. It had 50,000 watts of clear channel that covered most of the Eastern United States at night. We listened to that station way down in Florida.

Charlie set up an appointment with one of the most popular D. J.'s in the business — John Richbourg, better known as "John R. way down south in Dixie." One of his favorite sayings was "Get out of that back seat and act like somebody," or "Don't touch those knobs, those radio knobs, that is." His program was The Old Black Blues — and I'm talking about jamming on the back porch kind of music. He played artists like Jimmy Reed, Muddy Waters, B. B. King, Howling Wolf, and so on.

Now, most people thought John was black, but he was a big white dude that sounded black. Everyone that met him said, "You got a lot of soul for a white cat."

We walked into the studio that night and there he was, feet propped up on his desk spinning records. He said, "Of course, I'll play your record for you," and he did. Charlie and John were good friends. As a matter of fact, Charlie knew everybody in Nashville.

That record helped me and Bobbi get our foot in the door in Nashville, and it helped us meet a lot of influential people. It also got us booked on the Dick Clark "Caravan of Stars" show at the Memorial Auditorium in Chattanooga. That concert consisted of Lou Christie, John Fred and The Playboys, Gary Puckett and The Union Gap, and the Hollies from England. We did pretty good from that record, but we eventually moved on.

I continued to stay in close touch with Wayne and Charlie doing some more work at the Cinderella. Charlie had some great recordings that he played harmonica on that made him quite a bit of money. He landed the position as the band leader on the hit television show, "Hee Haw."

That little studio was very popular and a couple of big names that recorded there were Grand Funk Railroad and Neil Young. I haven't seen Charlie in a long time and he's probably retired by now. I recently found out he was originally from West Virginia, thanks to Google.

~

Later on the "Bobbi & The Blenders" made a return engagement to Leb's Pig Alley in Atlanta for a while. Again we stayed longer than expected, but we sure had a good time there.

On one trip, we found out that two of the Atlanta Braves baseball players had taken over the popular night spot. Joe Torre, the first baseman, and Clete Boyer, the third base player, had leased the club, but left all the original management in place. Joe Torre went on to manage the New York Mets and the Yankees. He was a great player and manager. Joe would slide mugs of beer down the bar to customers, some made it and some didn't, but it was all in fun.

Back then most games were playing during the day, not too many at night. Joe and Clete gave us free passes about forty rows up behind the batter's box. This is why I'm still a big Braves fan. We went to almost all the home games. Milo Hamilton was the radio commentator for the Braves and he would always wave and announce over the air that our band was playing at the club.

I got to meet a lot of big names in professional baseball. Most of them including the opposing team would come to the club that night after the game — it got pretty wild sometimes.

Hank Aaron, who broke Babe Ruth's home run record, was there most nights and I enjoyed chatting with him. He was a gentleman's gentleman. I saw him hit a ball clean into the upper deck at Fulton Stadium one time — the longest home run I'd ever seen.

I also got to meet Phil Niekro. He was one of the best knuckle ball pitchers in the league. When he would pitch a player by the name of Bob Uecker always caught for him. That was his job. He was one of the funniest guys I've ever been around. He would get up on the stage with us, tell jokes and sing *Miller's Cave*, which was an old country song. The audience loved it! Bob went on to do comedy and movies. He was best known as "Mr. Baseball." You could catch him on the Tonight Show with Johnny Carson.

I got to meet quite a few of the "stars" when they came to play the Braves in Atlanta.

One of my favorites was the manager of the Yankees, Yogi Berra. Not only was he a world series winning catcher, but was also a great manager. He coined the phrase, "It ain't over till it's over," which was made into a hit song by Lenny Kravitz in 1991.

Now, Yogi was a character, different from Bob Uecker, but still with a great sense of humor and very funny. At only five feet, seven inches tall, he played like a giant! One night, he and I were having a beer and he winks at me and says, in that gruff voice of his, "Get old Uke up on that stage and let him sing *Miller's Cave*." Well, of course we did, and Uecker put on a show! You could hear Yogi laughing above the crowd, egging Bob on. I wish I had that whole evening on video!

I believe the Yankees wore the Braves out at the Series that year. Yogi was one of the greatest! He was as popular as his team mate Mickey Mantle.

CHAPTER TWELVE
the Past, Present & Future

After Bobbi & The Blenders split up, I formed a group called "Past, Present, and Future." A four piece band with Pete back on bass, Shad Smith (from my old group the Big Brothers) on keyboards, and Larry Marks, a guitar player from New York.

I got a booking agent out of Milwaukee, Wisconsin, called Artists Corporation of America. They sent us out west to play a club in Pueblo, Colorado on the banks of the Colorado River. That river flooded the night spot while we were there. This was the furthest west I had ever been.

I remember there were a lot of Hispanics living in that area. They were friendly and most of the girls were good looking, I enjoyed dating a couple of them while I was there.

Pete and I decided to check out the Rocky Mountains. We went to Pikes Peak which is the highest mountain in that area at 14,000 feet above sea level, at the front of the Rocky's. I had seen the car races they had on the mountain track. I had an old station wagon we used to haul our band equipment and we wanted to see how long it took to make it to the top. There wasn't anyone there, so up that mountain we "tore" just as fast as we could. That was a trip a lot of fun. When we reached the top, although it was August and hot, there were piles of ice five or six feet high and it was COLD! At that altitude it was hard to breath, but man, what a view.

One weekend, Pete and I decided to go camping up in those mountains. We went to the Royal Gorge which has one of the highest swinging bridges in the United States, maybe even the world? People below looked like tiny ants. It was beautiful, although I think the Smoky Mountains in the fall is one of the most breathtaking places I've ever been. We had a great time camping, and it was the first time I ever heard a coyote howl. Good thing we didn't run into a mountain lion or bear.

Our agent sent us to Wichita, Kansas after this and what I remember most about Wichita was that it was where one of the "scariest" situations I've ever been involved in happened.

I met a young lady at the establishment we were playing and she invited me to her place after the show. Out of the blue, this dude charges in with a gun and pointed it straight at me. I had no ideal what was going on or who he was. The next thing that happened reminds me of the song by Lynyrd Skynyrd, *Give Me Three Steps* and *You'll Never See Me No More*. My lady friend jumps between this guy and me, screaming at him which was all I needed to break for the door and my car. Now, I was a fighter back in those days, but Mama didn't raise no fool. Unarmed and staring down the barrel of a pistol is quite a mismatch.

It turned out this guy was her on-again-off-again boyfriend that paid for the apartment. That was the last time I had anything to do with that crazy woman.

Chapter Thirteen
from Nashville to the Riviera

Pete soon got drafted into the Army, so I joined a band from Nashville called "The Fairlanes." We were more of a dinner and show type group. After signing up with ABC Booking Agency in New York, we had pictures made by Bruno of Hollywood. They do photography for a lot of actors and big names.

One of our gigs was a cruise ship to Spain, Portugal, Italy, and France. A four week cruise to the Mediterranean Sea area. Everything for us was paid, and we had free run of the ship. While at sea we performed, but when docked, we got to visit each country as a tourist.

When docked in France, we went to the famous French Riviera beach. I was not prepared for what I saw when we arrived. In every direction, as far as you could see, were French women with just bikini bottoms on. I thought I was dreaming or something. If you don't know, women go topless in France.

I met the coolest guy on the ship. He was a full blooded Apache Indian and he and his wife were returning from Europe to go to knife and fork school for a promotion in the Navy. He was to become a Chief (a rank in the Navy) but his grandmother kept telling him, "you no chief." He never could get her to understand that it was a promotion in the Navy. We had a great relationship coming back across the Atlantic.

One night the ship had a costume party and he came dressed as a cowboy. That really cracked everyone up.

He told me a story about one time when he was on leave and he was on his way back home to the reservation out West. He stopped for the night at a motel and decided to have a drink at the bar. He walked up to the bartender and ordered a drink. The guy told him they didn't serve alcohol to Indians (which was an out-dated law, but probably still on the books). His Apache blood started to boil and everyone could see it. He looked straight at that bartender and said, "I am in the United States Navy, and if I don't get a drink here, there won't be anything left of this establishment when I get through." Needless to say, he was served very quickly!

To this day I can't remember his name, but I'll never forget him and his wife. Hey, my Apache friend, if you happened to read this please contact me!

Being on a ship is like being in a small town. They have shops, an on-board radio station with a D.J., sports, and a doctor with a clinic. There are food and drinks everywhere, at any time of the day.

We were the top forty dance band and the ship had a full orchestra that played old classics such as Stardust, Moonglow, etc. We played poolside during the afternoon and in the dance lounge at night.

Wouldn't you know it, I was the only one in the band that got seasick. Those little pills didn't do anything for me, so thank goodness for the bartender. Whenever I got sick he made me a drink of peppermint liqueur and soda water. A shot of that and I would be okay for a while. I missed out on a lot of lobster and steak because of the nausea. As long as I was on deck outside I was fine, but down below, ugh!

The girls that worked on ship were like airline stewardesses. They must have been hand picked because they all were fine looking. One of the girls we became friends with knew all the ropes and helped show us around all the European cities. She knew how to bargain for deals, especially the Italian shoes. The girls from the ship always bought a bunch to sell back in the States.

Our new female friend was tall with long blonde hair and built, oh my! Her name was Honey Burns, but everyone called her Honey Buns of course.

In Italy the guys would pinch the girls on the butt which was the custom there. You should have seen the Italian boys leaning out of cars trying to pinch Honey's rear end.

On the trip back we hit a tropical storm. No one on board seemed to think anything about it. I asked the Captain, whom I got to know, about the storm and he said, "It's just the tail-end of some bad weather." He liked to dance, so he was always in the lounge. I teased him about who was driving the ship and let me tell you it was a huge one.

That evening around ten o'clock we were into our second set when the ship tilted a little from a wave. Pretty soon another wave hit, and I noticed the crew was beginning to tighten things up.

All of a sudden a huge wave hit us hard. We couldn't see it because of where we were in the lounge, but the ship rolled high to one side. Things started falling and the entire band and equipment went crashing into the left side wall of the room. All that was left was me sitting on my drum stool braced with my feet. No one in the lounge got seriously hurt, which was a miracle because all the glass, chairs, stools, people, and everything that wasn't bolted down got slammed against the wall.

Right above us was the main ballroom with the orchestra. I heard this loud boom and later found out it was the grand piano that hit the floor. The sax player fell and broke his arm. People were hurt all over the ship and the announcement came over the intercom for everyone to carefully make it back to their cabins.

The ship was back upright and a few more waves hit us, but the damage was done. The worst was over, but the clean up took all night. After we got our equipment back together, we had the rest of the night off. We and our Apache friend wound up on deck and watched the remainder of the storm. It was wild! Bob, our guitar player who couldn't swim, was scared out of his jock strap and proceeded to get himself a bottle of spirits to drink himself calm.

I sometimes wonder whatever happened to Honey Buns?

Chapter Fourteen
the Catskills & New York City

ABC Booking kept us up in the Northern states most of the time — New York, Massachusetts, Pennsylvania, etc. We worked in a resort in Greenwood Lakes, New York which is in the Catskill Mountains. That gig happened to be the same week of the famous three day Woodstock Festival, which was happening only forty miles away.

I hadn't heard much about it until it was over. All the big stars in rock & roll were there and I could have gotten in free because the fences were torn down by the fans. I still can't believe I didn't know about it because I sure would have been there.

That was just one of the many bloopers I've made along my journey.

Once, I was in Louisville, Kentucky during Derby week and didn't go. Another time I was in Augusta, Georgia during the Masters Golf Tournament and didn't go. Then, another time I was in Darlington, South Carolina during Nascar week — and didn't make that one either. I could have gotten in free, too. What was I thinking, or not thinking I should say?

I did get to play nine holes at The Masters golf course once when a club member invited me.

~

Later we were coming from Cleveland, Ohio where we had been hanging out with the television and Broadway star, John Davidson. We were playing the motel he was staying in. John was doing a show in town, and he would come in and catch part of our show regularly. He was a really a nice guy. We tried to get him to sing with us once, but he said rock wasn't what he could do.

~

Another time we had driven all night and gotten into New York around seven o'clock in the morning. Jim Miller, our saxophone player who was a big 'ole raw bone type of guy was driving. We were all worn out trying to get some sleep in the van while pulling a trailer. Along the way that night the worm gear in the steering column went "south." You could hardly turn the wheel, especially when stopped, and Jim was a strong guy. We had to be at our agent's office that morning, so we didn't have time to get the problem fixed. This was during the heat of summer — hot, hot, hot!

Most of us were trying to catch a wink when Jim arrived downtown. We were close to Times Square when he took a left hand turn onto a four lane one way street. All of a sudden someone hollered, "Jim, you're going the wrong way on a one way street."

We all woke up to see what was happening. Sure enough, Jim had taken a wrong turn on a one way. It just so happened all the early morning rush was stopped a block up for a red light, so Jim quickly turned right trying to get back onto the road he had turned from. What he did was get jack-knifed up against a parked car in the parking lane. With the steering almost impossible and Jim giving it all he's got trying to back up, then go forward. The sweat began to drip. NOW, here comes four lanes of rush hour traffic coming down on top of us. Yep, we completely blocked four lanes of rush hour traffic in New York City!

The very first car on top of us was a New York cab driver — uh oh! This cabbie sits down on his horn. Jim is pouring sweat and trying to get unjack-knifed and the cabbie is sitting on his horn. Well, it didn't take but a few seconds for Jim's temper to take over. He turned around and asked us pitiful like, "What am I going to do?" By then we were dying laughing and slid down in our seats, so all you could see was Jim which didn't go over well with him.

The cab driver was still sitting on his horn along with many other impatient drivers, when Jim opens the door and screams, "If you think you can do any better, you sons of bitches, get over here and do it." That stopped that horn real fast. By then, people that were on the sidewalk were stopping and we were drawing quite a crowd. This made Jim even more angry and embarrassed, so he yells at the onlookers, "Stick around and I'm going to sell tickets and popcorn." We were laughing so hard he threatened to kill all of us.

Inching back and forth, Jim finally backs all the way around and gets going the right way to the cheers of all that traffic that we had blocked. Jim says, "The first thing we're going to do is get this damn steering fixed. I'm plum worn out."

Once upon a time in Fort Wayne, Indiana, we were doing our "thang" when this dude walks up to the stage and politely asked if we would play *Red Roses For A Blue Lady* by Bobby Vinton. We said "Sorry sir, but we don't know that song." Thinking nothing about it, we continued playing, when about ten minutes later we heard a loud commotion near the front door. The bouncer had tackled someone and had him pinned to the floor. It was the red roses guy. He had gone to his car, gotten a pistol and came back through the door headed toward the stage. Thank heavens the bouncer grabbed him from behind before he could get to the stage. After wrestling the gun away, the cops were called in. Apparently, he was going to shoot one or all of us. Hey, I could have made up words if I'd known he wanted to hear the song that badly!

Chapter Fifteen
playing for the Military

We played for the military off and on during my musical career. This was during the Vietnam era of the 1960's and also in the 1970's after the war had wound down. The money was good, and with the guys and girls stationed on base we had a captive audience and always had a good crowd.

For one gig we flew down to Puerto Rico for a month and played for the Army, Navy, Air Force, and Marines. We arrived and got checked in with our military passes. They issued us a nice big van and we were free to travel anywhere on the island. It stayed around eighty degrees year round with a constant breeze. There were beautiful beaches and a rain forest. There were poor villages and wealthy areas.

We did Puerto Rico! Beaches, swimming, and sail boats from one end to the other.

One day we were having dinner in the officers mess hall and sitting across the room I noticed an officer that looked familiar. It turned out to be a friend of mine that I went to school with. I said, "Hal, what are you doing down here?" He told me he was a Navy pilot on a training flight from the States.

This same thing happened to me another time when I was up in Canada. One night while playing, I looked out on the floor and noticed a person I had gone to school with. People from the big city of Athens, Tennessee do seem to get around, I reckon. Turns out to be a very small world indeed.

Right before we left to go to Puerto Rico, our bass player quit. We didn't have time to find a replacement, let alone, teach him our songs. Bob was a talented guitar player. He could play guitar with his left hand and blow trumpet with his other, at the same time, of course.

I came up with an idea that took a little convincing for Bob and the rest of the band. He could play the Chet Atkins style guitar which is using all your fingers on the strings. We bought a cheap guitar at a pawn shop, drilled two holes large enough to place two bass strings on bottom, and the four others were the guitar strings. Being good at finger pickin' I knew he would figure it out.

Sure enough, he played the bass strings with his thumb and guitar strings with his fingers. He mastered it in no time, along with singing at the same time. Playing drums is like that to an extent. Your hands and feet are all doing something different while you are singing.

This is how we played for the remainder of our time together as The Fairlanes. We named that instrument a "soul-tar." Come to think of it, we should have made and sold those things.

While we were in Puerto Rico, we went over to Ramey Air Force Base to play a show which was on the far side of the Island. Going to the officers club we had to drive by the runway. I didn't count, but lined up on that runway was a row of B-52 bombers ready to take off. Each plane had two nuclear bombs loaded on board. That was what we were told, so I guess it was no secret. It was an eerie feeling, but I also felt a sense of pride, especially since I had dreamed of being a jet pilot in the Air Force at one time. The B-52s have been our work horse for years and it was something to see.

Right after that we were off to San Juan to play for the Marines birthday party. They had booked the whole upstairs floor of a beautiful hotel. They were stationed on the USS Guam which is a Navy ship. Now, Marines and Navy boys don't get along too well, especially when couped up on the same ship.

They sent a big Chinook helicopter to pick us up, equipment and all. They also had lined up some military girls to go. Needless to say, we had a loaded chopper.

After everything was loaded, we were given a set of head mufflers they called Mickey Mouse ears. That Chinook with the two large propellers was loud, very loud!

Their crew consisted of a pilot, a co-pilot, and two crew members, one of them from Tennessee. We hit it off right away, not realizing how excited they were, having this party.

We took off and followed the shoreline all the way to San Juan. Right about then our Tennessee buddy opens a box. Turns out it was a case full of Jack Daniels, quart size. They turned one up and proceeded to have a swig. The birthday party was on. They took it to the pilot cabin and passed it around there. Pretty soon I was beginning to get a little nervous.

It didn't take long before they weren't feeling any pain, including some of the lady friends on board.

The two crew members asked a couple of the girls if they wanted to come over to the half door on the side, so they could have a real good view of the beach and ocean below. When they looked out one of the marines kicked the door open and acted like he was going to push her out. She started screaming and he just pulled her back. Everyone was laughing their rears off.

Then the helicopter started dropping straight down. I started wondering if something was wrong with the chopper, and if we were going to crash? Everyone was just hanging on when I looked into the pilot cabin where the co-pilot was laughing. They had succeeded in scaring the crap out of us.

I was so glad to get off that thing, even thou I knew it was all in fun. By the way, the pilot was not drinking and had everything under control. Can you imagine what tricks of maneuvering they have to do in combat?

We set up and played for them until two in the morning. They had themselves quite a birthday, throwing water balloons at each other and on people walking below on the sidewalk.

The commanding Marine Officer was there and when the Navy Captain showed up they wouldn't let him stay. Makes you wonder how they get anything accomplished together.

Being out to sea a long time, I guess they have to let their hair down whenever they get a chance.

Our trip to Puerto Rico was a great experience.

Chapter Sixteen
playing the World's Fair

After my divorce, I tried to be with my daughter Michelle and son Ian regularly, but being in a professional road band made it tough. This is something you need to remember if music is your goal. I would drive all over the country to be with them — Summer breaks, holidays, etc.

I'm glad to say they have been successful in life, and married to great spouses. Ian lives in Columbia, South Carolina with my grandson Ethan, and with another one on the way. Michelle lives in beautiful Charleston, South Carolina.

Ian would watch me play and picked up drums naturally. I never showed him much, didn't have to. Being around his mother taught him to sing, so it's in his blood.

~

In the late 70's into the 80's we had a band called Smokey Jam which I will go more into detail about in the next chapter. This was the band that made an all out effort to get to the top. We got a booking at the 1982's Worlds' Fair in Knoxville, Tennessee — home of the Big Orange, Rocky Top, University of Tennessee Volunteers (of which I am a big fan). The theme of the fair was energy.

Oh by the way, my daughter Michelle graduated from the University of South Carolina, and with me being such a huge Volunteers fan we definitely have some fun during football season.

The gig was at the Australian Pavilion called the "Downunder Pub." It was on the bottom level with an open restaurant and pub complete with a stage and dance floor. It had no age limit because of the food and they served the Australian beer, "Fosters." It was the first time I had heard of it, and the alcohol content is a "little" stronger than American beer.

It was potent, and every night the Australian workers would have a beer drinking contest. I never saw them lose. Man, they could flat out drink beer. The cans are huge — they called them oil cans, and about one was all I could handle.

We were booked for the duration which was six months. It went down as one of the most fun times of my career. The place was packed seven days a week with people from all around the world. Different countries had pavilions, and the crowd ran around 85,000 a day.

People could just walk into the pub free, grab a table or stand. To this day, there's still a huge gold sphere on a high tower called the Sunsphere. You take an elevator up to restaurants and shops. It is painted with gold, even the windows.

Another thing left over from the fair is the outdoor pavilion next to a small lake. They had lots of events there, especially music. If you go through Knoxville on I-40 you can't miss the Sunsphere.

We got to be friends with so many people from every country that worked there. I started dating one girl that worked the Australian gift shop. Her name was Nicole and she told me she wasn't going back to Australia because the men in the United States were much nicer to women than the men in Australia. The reason is women in Australia out number the men about ten to one. That makes it hard for a girl to get a man and they know it. They treated women pretty bad back then, according to Nicole.

Nicole had a strong Australian accent and I could hardly understand her. I would tell her to speak English and she got a kick out of that. The funny thing was that Australian boys liked the American girls better. It must have been the hillbilly accent.

When we first started playing the fair we played thirteen hours a day, from noon until the wee hours of the morning. We got regular breaks and two long breaks. Around dinner time we got the longest break because at night we kicked it into high gear with rock and roll.

We came back in the evening backing a singer from Australia and he did all the typical songs from there — songs like *Tie Me Kangaroo Down, Waltzing Matilda, My Boomerang Want Come Back,* etc.

His name was Jim, and he was born in New Zealand but grew up in Australia. Everything was "hey mate" and "hi love." He was the show until after dinner. He was a really nice guy and we were all good friends. He told us a lot about Australia and we told him a lot about the United States. As a matter of fact the management and everyone was cool — definitely a fun time.

~

About three months into the gig at the World Fair, Jim had to go back home and I never understood why. I guess it was business. The manager decided to cut the hours to six at night with just our band. Seems word was spreading about Smokey Jam.

You could buy season passes and a lot of people did just that. The Worlds' Fair was the place to be in East Tennessee in 1982. People from all around Knoxville, and all the fair workers came to the pub. It became the "in thing" at night. With no age limit we drew teenagers, college kids, and people of all ages. You did have to be 21 to drink, but the young teenagers were there every night. A once in a life time opportunity for them, and the dance floor looked like the American Bandstand.

Ian came up from South Carolina to spend the summer months with me. I took him to the fair every day and he got quite a lesson from the foreign country pavilions. Being born into music he liked being with me at the fair, and it was the first time he got to listen to the music of our band.

He was thirteen and met this cute little fifteen year old girl who was there almost every night with a bunch of her friends and family. Boy, did he like her.

One day I dressed him up like a punk rocker and told him he was going to play drums on a song that night. I wasn't sure how he would do, but I had a feeling he would be alright. We got into our set, and after the place filled up, I told the audience my son was going to debut his drum playing. I went out front and counted off the song *Old Time Rock and Roll* by Bob Seger.

I knew he could play, but under those circumstances?

All I could say is he hit a home run! When we finished the song and he stepped off the stage, he was completely surrounded by the young people, especially the girls. He was in hog heaven!

60

When I took him back to South Carolina his mother called and said, "What in the world have you done to my child? He is acting different and not wanting to hang out with kids his own age." She forgot he is my child, too, and I guess I did spoil him a bit over the summer. Seems despite that summer he turned out to be a fine young man and father. I bet my grandson will be just as spoiled.

That same summer Van Halen came to Knoxville to play a concert. They showed up at the fair and we met most of the band members. Michael Anthony, who played bass, came into the pub while we were practicing and said, "You must be the band," and we chatted. Steve, our bass player, ran into Eddie Van Halen and asked him, "where is Valerie Bertinelli (his wife)?" Steve would rather see her than see Eddie — that's Steve for you. He also met David Lee Roth and tried to ask about music, but David only wanted to know where the girls were?

When the fair closed it was like a morgue and the whole city went into depression, especially the night life. Jim did try his best to talk us into coming to Australia when the fair was over. He said that we could make a lot of money because they loved American bands, especially the girls. We had other plans though with some original songs and recordings. The World's Fair was another once-in-a-lifetime experience.

I wonder what ever happened to Nicole?

Chapter Seventeen

taking it to Canada

Looking back, the fair was a big part of my life and career, but I need to go back to my place in this story.

Around 1970 our band, The Fairlanes were booked at the Goose Bay Strategic Air Force Base right across from the Canadian Air Force. The hunting and fishing was out of this world. Military brass would fly in just for that reason. As I've stated earlier, "No roads to Goose Bay — only mountains and wilderness."

It's also a radar site for the North Pole on top of a mountain, and the soldiers would stay up there for weeks. We watched the Northern Lights and they were beautiful. During the winter there are "white-outs" and no one is allowed outside. You can't tell where you are in the blowing snow, and your lungs would freeze. We were issued a Jeep, and stayed in the military barracks. We cruised around to see the lakes and mountains, a priceless adventure.

To get there we left our van in Long Island, New York and flew to Montreal, Canada in a military plane. There were only two flights a week out of that city and that was on prop planes. It took a while to fly that distance.

We had to layover in Montreal so we ate and hung out there for a few hours. The next flight was at night, so a couple of the band members went to the bar to have a toddy. When the boarding dock announced it was time to load, those two were nowhere to be seen. Nervously, I ran back looking for them, and when I got to the bar there they were, drunk as could be and not paying attention to the flight broadcast. My nerves quickly turned to anger and I drug those two out of there, only to find out the plane was on the runway. I found someone who could talk with the pilot and his answer was, "Sorry, you guys should have boarded on schedule." I couldn't believe what those two had pulled and I got really hot.

We had to wait for the next flight three days later, but the airlines put us up in a nice hotel. We called Goose Bay to get the band there to stay until we arrived. On the up side, we got to see Montreal.

Down the street from our hotel was a night club with a popular group out of Florida. It was "Wayne Cochran and The CC Riders" who had a hit called *Going Back To Miami*. We got to be friends and hung out with them for a couple of days. A few years later I ran into Wayne in Chattanooga.

When we finally arrived at the base we set up our equipment at the huge mess hall complex. It had two sections, one for the enlisted men and the other for Officers but only the one stage for both, so they mingled together. It had a room full of slot machines and it felt like a casino.

A lot of military girls came through there going back to the States. They came from Europe to Iceland and then to Greenland. From there it was Goose Bay, so there wasn't a shortage of females which suited the guys just fine. A lot of the girls were medical enlistees.

We played at the mountain radar site where the guys were starved for anything, being in such a remote station. Talk about a captive audience.

One night in November it came a terrible blizzard. It hit while we were playing, and the place was packed. Sure enough, it was a white-out and nobody was allowed outside. It didn't matter to us because we had everything we needed except beds. We played every song we ever knew at least twice.

We were confined for two days, so I finally got behind the stage curtains on the carpet and went to sleep. We ended up with a bunch of snow. I made that trip twice.

Just another spot on this Earth I would have never seen had it not been for the music.

CHAPTER EIGHTEEN
adventures in the Wild West

On a crazier side we had a booking in an all Mexican club in Kansas City, Kansas called Morie's Lounge. I had met a lot of Hispanics out West in Colorado, and any race was just people to us which is as it should be. God is color blind you know, as I have said many times. We had played many black clubs and every place we played treated us the same, and we did the same. I say that to lead you into this next story.

When we got there, we met Morie and his friends. He told us anything we needed would be no problem. The bouncer was a big tall Mexican whose name was Rabbit. He had a personality of a big 'ole teddy bear, but if he had to pick you up and throw you out he would. They liked the Motown Sound and we played a lot for them.

When they got to drinking it became party time. It reminded me of a bunch of Indians on "fire water." One night we were rocking out when all of a sudden we heard a "pop." Someone had fired a gunshot at another person. Everyone jumped up and turned tables over, and it seemed like everyone in there was packing a gun. Bullets started flying everywhere, just like in the western movies. It was a saloon-table-turning gun fight.

The whole band dived behind the organ, because it seemed like the safest place to be...I think? Then the cops came in and broke it up — thank goodness. It was if they were used to that sort of shenanigans. Some were hauled off to jail, and we resumed playing as if nothing had happened. Can you believe it? Not a single person got hurt. They must have been really bad shots. I did see one fellow get stabbed on another night though. It didn't kill him, but it was bad.

When we finished that gig and packed up, I planned to drive to Savannah, Georgia to see my kids before the next job. I told Rabbit where I was headed and he said, "Let me give you something to help keep you awake." I didn't know what that little pill was, but it was a long way and I took it.

I drove all the way to Savannah and didn't want to quit driving when I got there. That was the first time I had a truck driver aspirin which was a yellow jacket amphetamine. I thought I would never go to sleep.

Chapter Nineteen

no music like Family music

The Fairlanes finally split for various reasons. One of Jim's little girls had leukemia and he needed to be with her. She was around twelve years of age when she passed away. He was never the same after that, and he and his wife eventually divorced.

I began putting a new group together. Pete had gotten out of the Army and was back on bass. James from Savannah on sax, and I picked up a guitar player from Wisconsin. We went back to ACA Booking Agency and once again we were in the mid-western states.

Back home for a few days, my younger brother David had formed a band while in high school. He invited me to go to one of their practices. I couldn't believe how good they sounded.

I had been playing dinner music in suit and tie, and David's group were playing the younger style music. Stuff like Grand Funk Railroad, Jimi Hendrix, and such. It sounded exciting and a lot more fun than what I had been playing the last couple of years. I knew it would require a different type club, but our agent knew where to book us.

So in the early 1970's we decided to team up. David was out of school and anxious to pursue music. He also played drums so we formed a band called the "Past, Present and Future." David and I would switch from keyboard to drums and he took over half of the vocals, since I had learned to sing lead. David is extremely talented and that rascal could pick up any instrument and play it.

One of our gigs was an internationally famous restaurant in Milwaukee called Frenchy's. Presidents ate there, and they had a wild game menu with meat from all over the world, even wild African lion chops.

Frenchy, originally from France, was an older fellow with class running out his ying yang. He wore a tux and had a serious suntan from playing tennis daily. A true gentleman and a gracious host.

The lounge downstairs was called "The Bulldog Pub." Beer steins hung from the ceiling with celebrity names on them. I still have one to this day, and we even wrote a song about it.

You had to stand in line and wait for the doorman to let you in. About a block away was a nursing school and girls were everywhere. It took us our whole twenty minute break to reach the bar and back from the stage.

Frenchy liked us, so every now and then he would invite us up for dinner on him, anything we wanted. It was first class and delicious, and I had my first flaming cherry's jubilee. We played there many times, and once again definitely a story to write home about.

~

In Madison, Wisconsin we played a hotel lounge. It was a typical night club and one night while the owner was out of town, the manager, who was a cool dude, tells us after we finished playing that he was going to use the kitchen and cook steaks to have a private party. We got back to our motel late in the morning.

When we got to work that following Monday night the owner was back. David had a habit of putting his foot in mouth, and he bops up to this guy and said, "Man you should have been here the other night, we had a blast." The manager turned white as a ghost, not wanting the owner to find out about the party. He had to do some serious talking to save his job. Man, did we ride brother Dave about that, but we all got a big laugh out of the whole thing.

Our guitar player was a weird guy, at least he was while playing with us. He kept a jar full of I don't know what pills. One night I just about whipped his rear for smarting off to Pete, and it wasn't long after that he quit.

David had fooled around with a guitar now and then, so he wanted to play one for the band. He said he had been thinking about it for awhile. We went out, bought a guitar and started a crash course working with him. He was starting from scratch and we didn't have much time. We were playing a club circuit called the Left Guard which was owned by a couple of super bowl champs on the Green Bay Packers team. Fuzzy Thurston played left guard and Max McGee was wide receiver. They were nice guys, and we got to meet quite a few pro football players through their association.

It was a challenge for Dave to learn guitar and all our songs in such a short time. Our first booking with Guitar Dave was fast approaching. He literally slept with that guitar.

He is left handed, and I guess watching me when he was young, he played the drums right handed. That seemed to come natural and it gave him a wicked left hand on the snare drum. So, he took a right hand guitar, turned it upside down and played backwards making it difficult for someone to show him anything. I'm told Jimi Hendricks played that way, too.

I can remember guitar players sitting in our audience turning their head back and forth watching him play. When we took a break they would ask, "Are you playing that thing upside down?"

For about a month, poor David struggled and sounded rough but we managed to keep it going. It finally smoothed out and came together. Not just because he's my brother, but he is one of the finest pickers to come out of East Tennessee and can play any kind of music. He played the bass guitar the same way, upside down and all. You can hear his chops on our newly released album in this book. A collection of classic rock, all original by Smoky Jam.

Chapter Twenty

and then there was Smokey Jam

Sometime around the early seventies, Dennis Treadwell graduated from high school and joined our group. He played with David in his last band, and he owned a Hammond B3 organ with two Leslie speakers. I'm not sure where he got his nickname "Hob," but I think it means, "horny 'ole buzzard." All I know is, he has never denied it. I know for shore thou, he was born to play organ!

His keyboard and speakers were heavy, so his father gave us a six cylinder Ford van, and we managed to squeeze all the equipment and band members into that little van. It would be packed, and sometimes we drove one of our cars along, too. I had picked up a 1956 Chevy with only 55,000 miles from Fairlane Jim, and that's another car I wish I had kept. Hob added an electric piano and synthesizer, and he was set.

Pete had left the band, so along with Hob we added Jim French to play bass and invited James back on saxophone.

As I reflect back on those days, I had no idea it was the beginning of the most fun and accomplished years in my music career. We flat made some noise in the industry playing all kinds of music. It also was the beginning of our writing and recordings.

We played Columbus, Ohio and Lancaster, Pennsylvania, home of Amish farm country. If you have never been there it's really quite beautiful. They own hundreds of acres and their hand-built three story homes are exquisite. They are so white it nearly blinds you in the sun.

Amish roots came from Switzerland in a time of the Protestant reformation of the sixteenth century. Their religious ancestors were called Anabaptist (re-baptizers), because they baptized adults who had previously been baptized as infants in a Catholic or Protestant Church.

Their simple lifestyle makes me envious sometimes. Life can get too complicated and stressful. I guess my simple up-bringing is the reason.

After floating around the Midwestern states, we decided to come back to Tennessee and do our own gigs. Writing original songs was another reason. I had gotten enough experience playing for the military, it seemed to be the logical place to start.

I got on the phone and contacted some bases around the South. It wasn't long before we developed a circuit to perform. Playing gigs Friday through Sunday left a lot of time to write and work toward a record contract during the rest of the week.

I had remarried to a girl named Twila. We had a daughter, Megan Leigh, and she was and still is a daddy's girl. She gave me a fit raising, but Megan is my go to helper, and made me a Grandpa three times over. I love them all, and as a matter of fact I love every one of my kids and grandkids. Megan married a "cool dude." If not for a hip injury when he was very young, he would be playing professional sports today.

David and James were married (not to each other) so we settled back in Athens. It was time to get serious and make an all-out effort for that elusive hit record.

We also developed a local playing circuit and our fan following began to grow. We played high schools, colleges, night clubs, and so on.

On a recording trip to Nashville, we became friends with a songwriter/sax player who produced some songs we had written. That was when we decided to change the band name to Smokey Jam. Our bass player had dropped out, so our band consisted of Dave, Dennis, James, and myself.

Dennis learned to play bass on his synthesizer with his left hand and keyboards with his right. David helped out on bass guitar and this gave us bass, keyboards, guitar, sax, and drums with just four musicians. We played together for about ten years. A lot happened during those ten years.

When I got home from that recording trip, my wife met me as I pulled in. I could tell something was wrong before she told me the sad news. My mother had passed away from a heart attack. She was only 57 years old. I lost both parents way to early in life. My children hardly knew her and never knew their grandfather.

It has been hard for me, living without them all these years. I miss them, still do today. My older sister has filled that void a lot, though. I have always looked up to her as a role model, especially spiritually. Thanks Sis, I love you.

Hardly a day goes by that someone doesn't ask me, "Didn't you play with Smokey Jam?" or "Do you guys still play?"

We developed a good reputation and a loyal following. People would go where ever we performed. The gigs were assured of a good crowd and that would get you a lot of bookings.

We met a guy in Knoxville, Joe Overholt, that owned a recording studio and a company that built sound boards. We used his studio a couple of times and liked the sound. We negotiated a deal to buy a board and build our own studio. Joe sold us the components, and I put them together, not realizing what I had gotten into. Hundreds of pieces to solder and screw together. It took me six months to complete. Finally, in the basement of my Mom's house we had a studio, and we began our serious recordings.

During the sixties and seventies, drugs became the "hip" thing. A lot of people were into downers, such as pot, quaaludes, and even heroin. Not me, I could get down naturally. I needed something to get me up though.

Diet pills were popular, and doctors were writing them to people who wanted to lose weight. They made you speed up. I was too skinny for a prescription, but as I've said, being in a band, people will give you anything.

Playing in a rock band does require a lot of energy and I would lose five pounds playing a four set gig. It was mostly fluids, but look at most hard rockers, they are slim. A diet pill and two fingers of gin got me up and ready to play. More about this later.

The military circuit we were working consisted of Tennessee, Georgia, Alabama, and Florida. Playing Red Stone Arsenal Army Post in Huntsville, Alabama was one of our best jobs. We played for the officers, enlisted, and N.C.O. clubs. The money was good, and we were there about once a month.

Huntsville has the Space Museum, and it's all about NASA and the rockets. I've been there quite a few times, a must place to visit.

CHAPTER TWENTY-ONE
Weddings and Rattlesnakes

About this time Hob met a girl and they fell for each other. A sweet gal whose name is Cathy, and they married and still together today.

When the wedding date was set the guys and I got together and threw a bachelor party the night before with some tricks up our sleeves. We got a motel room, hired a dancer, and bought a bottle of tequila. We also brought cigars and a bottle of molasses. Molasses you say? I'll explain in a minute.

The bachelor party was in full swing, the dancer was doing her thing, and we told Hob we had tequila. We told him we were going to do "shooters," but we had two tequila bottles. One was alcohol and the other was water. The little glass for him was tequila, but the rest of us were drinking water. We fired up those cheap cigars, filling the room with smoke and it was sickening.

Pretty soon Hob had just about enough, so we got him to lay down. When he was half asleep, we poured molasses all over his hair which was sort of 'afro' style. You can imagine what a mess that was.

The next morning, hung over and trying to collect himself for the wedding, Hob spent most of that time washing his hair, over and over. He finally got the molasses out, but it left his hair frizzy and standing straight out.

Cathy had a short hair style, too, and when they stood in front of the Preacher it was hilarious looking. Cathy with her short hair and Hob with his frizzy hair, oh my! I think his parents were a little upset with us, and I couldn't blame them. Needless to say, Hob swore to get us back. It was one for the books or should I say, "this book."

We had the privilege of playing for the Army's two hundredth birthday celebration. The main party was at Fort Benning in Columbus, Georgia and I think it's one of the oldest. They had two bands booked for the week long event. Starting with parades and a circus like atmosphere, we were the rock band to perform in the dance lounge at the Officers building, wearing white and all. We were "hot" in those tuxedos playing rock and roll.

The other band was the Buddy Morrow Orchestra, and they played in the ball room for older people. One of Buddy's hits was Night Train, and I enjoyed their big band sound.

All the top brass was there, including General Westmoreland who was over the Vietnam program. The highlight of the whole shindig, President Ford was there, which makes two Presidents I have seen. The other was President Ronald Reagan, who came and spoke at the courthouse in Athens, Tennessee. I've never seen so many people downtown in all my life.

Another popular place for us to play was Fort Rucker, Alabama. We played most of the civilian lounges around that area. Enterprise is the bowl weavel capital of Alabama with a statue and all. Opp, Alabama is the rattlesnake capital and has the biggest diamondbacks. You would just have to see it to believe it. Opp has a week long rattlesnake rodeo with glass wagons to put the snakes in. Back then, it was twenty five dollars a snake, and the guys would go out and catch as many as they could. They would "milk" the venom and cook some up to eat. Those wagons were loaded with snakes.

We got to be good friends with some of the locals who came to the club every night. We booked a club for two weeks, and never had to stay in a motel. Most were single with their own place and room to put the band up for the engagement. Having to work a day job they were glad to see us leave.

Once, one of those good 'ole Bama boys said, "Come over here and let me show you something." He had a large barrel, took the lid off and said, "Look here." We walked toward that barrel and our buddy kicks it at us. Out of the thing slithers a couple of big diamondbacks. You should have seen us high jumping backwards, and 'ole buddy was dying laughing.

We would later get those boys back. We invited them up to our stomping grounds in East Tennessee one time. We had white water rafts, so we took them down the Chattooga River. A river that can be very dangerous — where the movie "Deliverance" was filmed.

We were into white water, and rode most wild rivers around. Our buddies had never been on rapids and they were petrified. One had a bottle of scotch and it was gone in no time. We got them back and then some. A lot of people have gotten killed on that river. To us Tennessee boys it was a great day!

Fort Rucker was a helicopter training post for our troops and allies. One day driving by the airfield, I saw this chopper coming in for a quick landing. They train their soldiers to come down fast, pick up the rescue, and off again to avoid shots from the enemy.

A teacher and a student was training and as he came in I could tell he wasn't going to level off just right. When that Huey Chopper hit the ground, parts flew everywhere. A hospital chopper came and picked up those two, but neither was badly injured. They were lucky.

On Saturday night, after we finished playing, we headed off to Panama City, Florida. We would stay up the whole time, just hanging out at the beach until time to go back to the club and play that coming Monday night. We all had a nice suntan after that gig.

Back in those days you could buy ephedrine pills over the counter. I would get them to stay awake, and they came in handy if you needed to drive or study. I would take one to keep my energy level up playing drums, and great if you wanted to diet. They have been taken off the market without a prescription.

Another crazy thing I would do was take a primatene asthma tablet to speed up, and it's sort of like the adrenaline you get in an epi-pen, which I now keep close by for bee stings. With a shot of tequila you are definitely awake. Remember me saying, "I needed something to get me up?" Just one of many stupid things I did when I was younger.

Chapter Twenty-Two
finally cutting some Tracks

During the Seventies a lot of young people grew into adulthood listening to Smokey Jam, and the loyal fans kept increasing. We entered band battles and usually won. By the early 1980's we had written enough songs to record an album. In the beginning, Dave and I wrote separately, then later moved toward working together which worked out a lot easier. The album plans were made and the songs were selected to begin the recording process. This took quite a while because we recorded songs in different studios.

We had met William Lee Golden through a mutual friend. William Lee is the long haired singer in the Oak Ridge Boys group. He lived in Nashville, and his sons had a rock band. He is a nice guy that likes Indian stuff. Some of his house is decorated in that style, and he has a beautiful white teepee in the yard. It was huge, and he slept in it occasionally.

We were at his house a few times and he was always gracious. Ron Fairchild played piano for the Oak Ridge Boys, and owned a recording studio in Nashville. All the musicians in the band were good, so we recorded two of the album songs in Ron's studio. North Georgia Rambler and All In Love Again, featuring their sax player.

Two other songs were cut in Nashville at Mercury Studios, produced by a killer bass player, Steve Schaffer — *I Want To Love The Night Away* and *I Got Love*.

We played the scene in Nashville at most of the hot spots, including the famous Blue Bird Cafe where many a star were discovered. I reflect back to those days and I realize we were pushing rock in a country and western city. Playing the Blue Bird, people looked at us like "What is this band doing?" We should have taken our material to New York or Los Angelos. Let that be a valuable lesson to remember.

I met Chet Atkins while playing a Brenda Lee birthday party. I met Dallas Frazier at one of the Nashville clubs. His big hit was Elvira by the Oak Ridge Boys. I also did a session with Don Tweedy, who was our sax player's brother-in-law. He did a lot of record producing. He did the arrangements for the huge hit, *Ode to Billy Joe,* by Bobbie Gentry. He also was very good friends with Henry Mancini.

On one session with Don, the engineer was Scotty Moore, Elvis Pressley's guitar player, who told us many stories about "The King."

Chapter Twenty-Three
the Nashville Rat

A friend and I came up with a cartoon character named "The Nashville Rat." He had drawn the "Rat" and I wrote a children's book and song about the character. We then proceeded to search for a backer to produce it. Too bad Shark Tank wasn't around at that time.

We started taking in partners to help pay for the project, and got it copyrighted. This led me to Sam Walton's vice-president of marketing for WalMart, Ron Loveless, who I became good friends with.

We had gotten a stuffed animal made of that little goober, so Ron advised me to get the song, book, and stuffed rat packaged together. If we would get some sales and create a track record, he promised that he would write me a six months guarantee of WalMart shelf life. THAT COULD HAVE BEEN HUGE!

We still didn't have it quite there yet, so Ron told me to contact this record producer in Nashville, Don Goodman. He wrote songs for big name stars in country music.

When I met Don, he wanted to rewrite the song and brother did he — he changed it completely. It was what we needed for the project. We recorded it with a couple of studio musicians that later worked with Garth Brooks. That song could have been a hit if only it had been promoted right. The whole thing could have been successful if not for too many

partners with too many ideas. It got so entangled in legality, that the project got lost in it all and it became another project that "could have been." Let that be another lesson you need to remember. Keep your business partners to a minimum.

Chapter Twenty-Four
7-inch boots & River Raft Races

We opened for a popular group that had a hit record called Vehicle. The group was "The Ides of March" and the concert was at Cleveland State Community College in Cleveland, Tennessee in the mid 1970's. It was Smokey Jam's first warm-up show for a name act. We thought we would turn it on and make some noise.

We did our thing and felt pretty good about it until Ides of March came on. We got a lesson about "big time" real quick. They were good and it helped us later on.

Knowing what had to be done, we put our original songs in concert style. Then we had a stage costume made and wore seven inch high boots which was a little like the band Kiss. David played barefooted, and those boots made me almost seven feet tall. It was hard to play drums in those things but we looked good.

After hooking up with a D. J. friend of ours that owned a radio station which covered East Tennessee, he put us on a couple of big shows. One was a four wheel drive drag race on a farm outside Knoxville. I had never seen such a thing. There were trucks, Jeeps, and everything else that had four wheel drive.

The track was dirt, and we set up next to it on a flat bed wagon. It was a weekend in summer and the place was packed. We had a shed for a dressing room to put those outfits on, and it was hot with no air conditioning or fans.

I had some tequila, so I took a swig right before we went on. When I walked out in the sun I had spots dancing in my eyes. Thank goodness I got to sit down on my drum stool. It took a few minutes to get my bearings. Later I laughed about it. Tequila and hot sunshine will do a number on you.

Here's the funny or I should say sad part about that ordeal. There we were playing and they would crank up those four wheelers racing right by us. The dust and dirt from those vehicles covered us and our equipment completely. It was a mess and took days to get the dirt out of all our equipment, especially Hob's organ.

Another deal our friend put together was the Clinch River Raft Race that lasted all weekend. Everyone came with campers and tents. Not only was it a race, but they gave prizes to the most creative or ridiculous looking raft. Some were hilarious.

The Clinch comes out of the Cumberland Mountains in East Tennessee and empties into the Tennessee River. You talk about cold! It made you think the river had ice cubes in it. I guess thats why so much "fire water" was consumed.

There were other bands that played, mostly bluegrass, but we were the headliner. We didn't get much sleep, but all you had to do was take a dip in that cold water to become instantly awake. That was one wild and crazy weekend.

Hanging out in Nashville so much led us to a big time promoter, Joe Sullivan. His company was called Sound Seventy Productions. Guitar Dave somehow made contact with him and sent some of our original songs. Joe liked what he heard and told us to give him a shot, so we put everything on hold to see what would workout with him.

During this time I came down with a ruptured appendix and Dave had to hire another drummer for about six weeks. Joe sent a rep to hear Smokey Jam live in Chattanooga. With little time to practice with the new drummer Smokey Jam was not at our peak, and we think our chances of signing were weakened.

The southern rock band, Wet Willie with their hit song Keep On Smiling, was on Capricorn Records at the time. Capricorn was going out of business, and Joe had a chance to sign Wet Willie. It came down to us or Wet Willie, and because they were already established, Joe took them. We had come so close!

After signing with Sound Seventy, Wet Willie played a concert in Sweetwater, Tennessee and we warmed them up. By then we were a seasoned concert group, and when we cranked up they came out and watched our show. We let the hammer down, and I think they were impressed. The crowd was yelling our name and that felt good.

Joe booked for the Charlie Daniels Band and some other great groups, too. He wanted us to warm up more of his concerts. We declined, because we wanted to look for another record producer, since Joe wasn't signing anybody else on at the time.

A couple of Athens businessmen turned the old movie theater downtown into a hot dance club called the Stage Door Club. It became the place to go in the area, and it held enough people to bring in some name acts.

Smokey Jam was a regular because we had our following and we always packed it out. By then we had our concert show fine tuned, and still did cover songs. One song was *Train Train* by Blackfoot. Toward the end of that selection, the crowd would holler, "GIVE THE DRUMMER SOME!" I would make a train sound, and the other band pickers, with drum sticks in hand, joined me on my drum riser. Guitar Dave on toms, Hob on big tom, James on cymbals, and with all four playing a drum solo it was a crowd favorite.

Hob took a ax handle and guitar strap, attached them to his Arp Synthesizer so he could stand up to play. This was before they came out with keyboards with handles. Who knows, somebody could have taken our ideal to a music company? We were ahead of our time with that one.

One Saturday The Grass Roots played the Stage Door Club. They had many top forty hits. We were chosen to "warm them up," as its called. Each band would play two shows and we were first. Smokey Jam fired both barrels and when Grass Roots played their show, the crowd with all our fans started chanting "Jam, Jam, Jam." I really felt bad for them because their music was sort of "bubble gum." Not only that, they argued with each other while on stage and made things more embarrassing for themselves.

One group that went over well at the Stage Door Club was Wild Cherry — *Play That Funky Music*. We missed that gig because we were performing out of town that weekend.

Chapter Twenty-Five
good things don't last Forever

Striving to land a record deal, we picked up local jobs to stay in the recording studio working on originals. A couple of spots we played turned out to be classics. One was a small room at the Scottish Inn Motel in Athens. A little stage was built and presto, a small dance lounge that held a few people. The place would be packed with standing room only every weekend.

The parking lot would be full, so people would take turns coming in and out. Somehow it all worked and everyone had a ball. One reason was the age limit had dropped to eighteen. With a big college in town the students turned out, and that meant lots of young single girls.

The other place was a country club outside of the city limits by the name of the Chestue Country Club. We had lots of room upstairs and downstairs. You could purchase a mixed drink at this place. The police were called a few times by neighbors complaining about us playing too loud. Now, isn't that being narrow minded? We played Tuesday, Friday, and Saturday nights. It was always packed with our following and college students.

Another fun place was in Gatlinburg, Tennessee. Resort areas always paid the most money, and they put you up in a motel room. Gatlinburg is always packed with tourists from everywhere, and was a hot spot for spring breakers.

We always got free passes to a lot of the rides and shows, too. I got to know some of Dolly Parton's family while we were at the Holiday Inn lounge.

I really loved all the car shows that were held in the area, and hiking all the beautiful trails in the Smoky Mountains.

Eventually, I got into drugs and alcohol because people would offer them to me for free. That is the biggest pitfall of being in professional music. You start thinking you can handle just taking a little and before long it becomes more important than the music, more important than anything. It takes a hold of you and you are taking more and more. It will ruin you in more ways than one. Money, marriage, family, and so on. I've always said it was best for me to not get a record deal or make big money. I'm not sure at that time if I could have handled it. That temptation has been fatal for some musicians, and I know someone up there that had other plans for my life.

By now we had recorded enough songs for three albums or more. We completed the first and named it 'Wagon Of Freedom.' I have added the second album to this book for all you classic rock fans. It's called 'Resurgence.'

As we grew older the rigors of travel, marriage, and kids started taking it's toll on Smokey Jam. We had put so much effort into that elusive recording contract and it finally came to a crossroads.

Hob and James decided to drop out to pursue another direction in their lives. Music had been all we knew up until then. David and I found a bass/guitar player to keep going — a three piece band. We played together for two more years, but we could tell the end was coming.

Smokey Jam had a great run with lots of good times. It was the best band I ever played with. I hope you enjoy the songs which are new "old classic rock and roll."

Sometimes, today we get together with four other singer/musicians and play once or twice a year. A lot of fun, but I don't miss setting up all that equipment and stuff.

~

When we closed the book on Smokey Jam I formed a country/rock band, and we called ourselves "Four Wheel Drive." We played in and around Jellico, Tennessee. Then, the age to drink was still eighteen, and across the border of Kentucky it was totally dry. In other words you couldn't even buy a beer. This made Jellico a boom town for music lounges and dance halls. I stayed and played that area for a year or so.

One night we were playing the Am-Vets Club and I saw this girl on the dance floor shaking her junk. From behind my drums I made eye contact with her. She had a beautiful smile, and I thought, "I've got to meet this girl." When we finished our set I chased her down and we talked for a moment, then I bent down and kissed her. It really caught her off guard.

I look back on that night and it was what I've heard, love at first sight. Christina Marie Besey became my girlfriend and two years later we were married. Both of us had been divorced. I had never been able to hold a marriage together before, but this past year (2015) Chris and I celebrated our twenty-eighth wedding anniversary on February 15th. We were going to be married on Valentine's Day, but I had a mean case of stomach virus and we had to wait until the next day.

Chris had a son by her ex, and I had custody of my third child. Bradley Wayne and Megan Leigh are both the same age, so we had an instant family at home when we got married. It was like having twins, and they are very close to this day. Neither took the music route but Brad can build a house from the ground up and is a really good artist. Megan is one of those that didn't have to open a book and still make straight A's. She is helping me with this book. I should have studied harder in English.

It wasn't long before my fifth and last child was on the way. A blonde headed boy, and everybody teased me about it. There was no one in my family with blonde hair. Finally around eight years old his hair turned brown. He is definitely a Passmore, though. Jesse Carmel is learning to play drums and bass. He is also an artist concentrating on creating computer game characters.

Megan has three children — Shalia, Javianna, and Nashon. Brad has one, Jasmine, and my son Ian has one son, Ethan, with another on the way. I have so much joy with my grandchildren.

You can say, "I met my wife in a bar!" She is my best friend and soul mate. I made a vow to give this marriage my best shot, and it's been amazing — so far, so good. Up until this point I had been a terrible husband, but I still considered myself a good father.

~

For those who don't know, there is a tourist attraction outside Williamsburg, Kentucky called Cumberland River Falls. What is unique about this the huge waterfall there is, on a clear full moon night you can see a rainbow or actually it's a moon-bow. People come from everywhere to see it. I've tried several times but it's always been cloudy and blocked out the moon. I hear it's beautiful and only one other like it in the world. The other one that I know of is in Africa.

Once when Chris was swimming at the top when she was a child, she got caught in the swift current and headed toward the falls. It would have been a sure death if she had gone over, but thank Heavens a man saw her and pulled her to safety. Chris tells me this story every time we're there. Oh, and she tells me that I repeat myself as often as she does. I guess that's a part of getting older.

Chris' mom and dad moved to Williamsburg from Monroe, Michigan when she was a young teenager because they were tired of the snow and ice. They liked the Cumberland Mountain area and settled there. Chris said it was like going back in time. Her parents shopped at a country general store that carried everything from food to clothes.

Living into their nineties, her mom and dad wanted to be cremated, so we spread their ashes together in the falls area. A beautiful resting place.

Williamsburg is a small town with Cumberland College in the heart of the city. It's definitely coal mining country. Kentucky, like Tennessee, grows some of the purest marijuana this side of Columbia. Probably a number one cash crop in the area.

That gig at the Am-Vets Club where I met my wife was run by two brothers. It had a sign on the front door that read no guns or drugs. Well, there was a bullet hole in that metal door and almost every one carried a gun. You could find just about any drug made, also. It was a wild place that payed good because it stayed packed and really never closed.

One night I had a little too much to drink and the next day my head was splitting. I ask one of the regulars if he had something to help my hangover. He gives me this pill and said it would do the trick. I had to get another drummer to play for me that night. That dummy had given me a Thorazine tablet which is for mental problems, and I could not wake up. I should have been the one nicknamed Dummy!

There was a large show room downstairs used for big name acts. We played there off and on for about a year. Around 1984 someone blew that building to kingdom come for reasons I never found out.

Along this time Chris and I were dating steady and I started thinking it was time to put my sticks down. After all, I played on top of the world and now I was in coal mining bars. I had pretty much run my music race. Drinking and popping pills got to be more important than picking up those drum sticks. We had two children and it was time to think about my family and get my priories right.

Eventually we ended up in Etowah, Tennessee and I was asking myself, "What am I going to do now?" Music was all I had ever known.

Chris and I got married, got jobs and started the next phase of our lives. I taught her to sing and we did a glorified D. J./live show on the weekends, so I wasn't completely out of music. I guess once music is in your blood you never really leave it.

My attention turned to writing songs, children's books, and inventing various items to be patented. Brother Dave started another band locally, and kept the recording studio going. Dave and I again, got into writing and recorded some country music. I played drums with his group, Main Street, for about a year. We only played a Saturday now and then.

I finally stopped drinking and have been clean and sober for almost twenty years now. I've found out music is so much more enjoyable sober. Music is such a high itself, a world all it's own. That's how it was when I first began. Somewhere along the way, amidst all the booze and drugs, I lost my vision.

As good as my oldest son is, I discouraged him from doing what I did and he listened. Thank you, Lord!

I got a job driving an ice delivery truck. By doing that I learned to drive a tractor, trailer rig, although I never applied for my CDL license.

Charleston, South Carolina took a direct blow from hurricane Hugo and my company boss got the idea to rent a Ryder big rig to take a load of ice to Charleston. The tractor was a cab-over which wasn't heavy enough to carry such a load. There was a shortage of ice and it was hot down there.

The boss asked me if I could drive it and my reply was, "of course." But to tell you the truth, I'd never been behind the wheel of one. A friend and I took it around the block, got ready to go and left around six o'clock that evening. We were told to dodge the weigh stations, so we went through the Smoky Mountains. It started raining and the trailer was pushing the cab all over those curvy roads. I got "schooled" real quick in a short amount of time on how to handle a rig like that.

We spent a week on that trip, and had to trade the tractor for another because of mechanical problems. Ryder gave me a "Cadillac" to pull that heavy trailer. It was a "General" which was big and heavy. It made the rest of the trip so much easier.

I often thought about driving a truck for a living, but never got around to it. With baby Jesse, we decided to stay put.

David was pretty much in the same boat. He started finishing sheet rock and wound up getting a Tennessee contractors license. I joined him with the sheet rock, and now we build houses from the ground up. We must have gotten that from our dad and grandfather who were house builders. I really enjoy finishing a house because it satisfies my creativity where music left a void.

One day Dave wanted to know if I would like to work in Florida. Charlotte County had gotten slammed by Hurricane Charlie and some friends of ours were down there making really good money.

I wound up there for a year, and made more money than I've ever made. Most of the work was for the rich who had good insurance. They didn't care the cost — just when can you do the job.

I took my wife and youngest son with me and we did Florida — Disney World, Miami, the beaches, Busch Gardens, Universal Studios, Everglades, and the Keys. I knew we would never get that opportunity again, although I had played all over the state in younger years I really hadn't seen much of the state, and I had the money to do it right this time.

We came back to Tennessee after we cleaned up most of the damage from the hurricane and bought a scenic piece of property in McMinn County. Chris and I designed and built a moderate house to settle in, but things could change down the road. That's how life goes.

I'm building houses and driving a school bus now. Sometimes I play or sing in church, and it seems some days like I've lived two lives. I have been more places, met so many different people, and done things that this Tennessee Hillbilly would, as I have already stated, never done if not for the music.

I often wonder — was it a good or a bad thing? I do have five children and five grandchildren, with another one on the way, that I love dearly. I do know that musicians never die, they just play into the sunset.

On a serious note, a rock musician is like the old blues pickers, you can roll until your 100. If you don't think so, just look at the Rolling Stones.

Chapter Twenty-Six

advice for Future Musicians

How do you make it in the music industry and yes, I'm referring to becoming a 'name' or 'big star?' Do you want to be a 'hit' singer or a 'big time' musician? Maybe your interest is in writing or producing? What about a recording engineer? There are many things you can do chasing that elusive big time rainbow. I have done all these things in my music career. A musician, singer, producer, engineer, booking agent, drum teacher, songwriter, and most everything else concerning music.

The first thing you have to figure out and make a decision about is, "Do you have a natural feel for music?" If you aren't born with that natural talent it's best to be a 'roadie.' A Roadie is someone who works for bands driving, or setting up equipment. They travel with the band, and live the band life, but they don't actually play in the band. Don't let a relative or friend try to convince you otherwise, just because they want it for you. Remember, everyone thinks they are music experts. Do serious soul searching and know for sure. If you don't, it can be a very depressing letdown.

If you have the talent and the drive to stay with it, the best thing you can do is write, write, write. They will tell you in places like Nashville, "We've got a thousand pickers, just give me one good song."

If you're a musician 'sleep' with your instrument. Live and breathe your instrument. You are only as good as the time you spend practicing, and the same goes with singing. Lessons will help speed things up if you've got a good teacher. Even if you have a good voice, lessons can help you to train your voice. You hear often of singers that have strained their vocal cords and have to stop singing for a while to let it heal. Voice lessons can help you save your voice.

Listen to everybody who is accomplished and try picking up at least one good 'lick' from them. Practice what you heard and incorporate it into your style, instrument or vocal. The secret, as I have mentioned, is concentrate on writing and recording. Take your songs to producers and if they hear something, they will pitch it to an established name or maybe want you to record a demo. Treat it like a business, not a party. Producers and record labels can be researched on the computer.

Form a group and play anywhere you can. If you can make money it will help the cause. If just being a 'road group' is what you want, stay on top of the forty count down. If you can't dance to it don't play it. It's also good to have some of the popular old classics in your repertoire. A variety is always a good thing, and try pleasing as many as you can. Play what your audience wants, not what you like.

Resort areas are the best places to play and they pay the most. Tourists are looking for things to do and spend money. A good booking agent is a positive. In the long run the money you pay for them is worth it. Let them worry about finding gigs and you work on your music. There again, find them on Internet.

Create an advertising package with a catchy name and logo for your band. Have a professional take pictures. List everything you've done, places you've played, and performers you have worked with. Put a good song list into the mix.

Be creative with what you wear to separate yourself from the audience. Be different, and wear a suit if it helps — a cool one.

Pick songs that have a lot of harmony vocals because it's very impressive. Always, and I mean always, smile and move on stage. Act like you're having a good time and this requires practice, but it will separate you from other bands. After all, you are entertaining and people listen with their eyes.

Someone in the band, who is a good speaker and out front, needs to MC for you. Talk to the audience, watch them and flow with how they are responding. It's important that you work the crowd. Be serious and treat it like a job.

If you stay together and not change musicians constantly, Las Vegas is looking for good road bands!

Last piece of advice — don't let alcohol or drugs become more important than the music because it will destroy your hard work. Having that talent is a gift, and you are living your life in a unique world. Only an entertainer can feel that 'high.' Treasure it.

If your desire is to someday be in the Rock & Roll Hall of Fame or receive a Grammy for best new country artist — and let's not forget Gospel's Dove awards, too. Here are a few things to remember: You better have patience, talent, and a lot of being at the right-place-at-the-right-time luck. If you are one of the few that possess that kind of tenacity, then you owe it to yourself — let the world hear you!

As I have deliberated, the best way to accomplish this is write and perform your own original music. You may want to play with a band and do cover music to pay the bills, or maybe you can just concentrate on your own goals which is best. If you do the cover thing do it part time and devote the rest to originals.

One important thing to song writing is to listen to what's hot today and figure out where it's going six months from now. There is a pattern to this which you can learn if you study it enough. If you do this you'll have a head start.

Find places to showcase your stuff. Places where the 'right' person will hear you. An example is the Bluebird Cafe in Nashville. A lot of performers have been discovered there (and not just country acts), and there are those kinds of show rooms in every major city. Take some time and research it. Don't do what we did, and that was playing rock in a country showroom — it won't work.

Let everybody who is anything hear your work. As I've said, you've got to have some luck being at the right place at the right time. Analyze and create from artists that are producing more than one or two successful songs. Think of a line, a 'hook' as you will, that is melodic and build the verses and bridge around it. A personal experience is usually the easiest, but there are other ways to get ideas for songs. Once you figure out a workable formula it gets easier. Write songs that have a good feel and think radio music because 'radio-feel' is what opens doors.

Social media has done wonders for up and coming artists in today's world. You can lay down a song and create a simple video without spending much money. It's simple to get it on You Tube. All you have to do then is get as many people as you can to view it and share it. One way is Facebook and if you get it to go viral, lookout! It's been done quite a few times.

Work up an original show and perform everywhere you can. Make sure you have a good show to watch and dress the part. Find producers and labels to send your songs to. This means you will need to have your songs copy written in Washington. It's not that expensive, and once again find the information on Google. If you don't, anyone can steal your song. You'll also want to sign up with BMI or Ascap. It's cheap and they collect your royalties once it's on radio or television.

If you write a song that some big name artist wants to record, let them. You can collect quite a large percentage on writer's royalties if it's a hit. Your odds are much better going in that direction, and you've got the door wide open. If you can find a financial backer or someone with money that believes in you, get a lawyer and work out a deal. There are good music lawyers and they are easy to find. I have a real good friend in Nashville that's one, and he knows music inside and out. Be careful, and don't give too much away.

A person that has money and wants to invest in most anything is called 'Angels.' These people are out there, but they are hard to find. When a producer says he will record you and your song for a large amount of money to get you a record deal, be careful. Some of these people prey on your excitement just for your money, and no one can promise you a 'hit.' Only a legit record label can do anything of this nature.

One negative thing you'll probably hear is that there is no more room for another successful entertainer. Take that with a grain of salt. There are new stars breaking into the industry every year.

Don't be discouraged by failure either. Some of the largest stars in the music industry have had failure upon failure. Garth Brooks and Taylor Swift were turned down by just about every label in town before they finally got their big break.

The music scene is divided into 'clicks' in most major recording cities. You have to study and research how to become friends with a particular music group you're trying to be a part of that can benefit you.

I said it's tough, but if it was easy everyone would be a star. Patience has to be a big part of your goal, so grab the challenge and enjoy it. Don't take no for an answer. Hang in there and never give up.

Chapter Twenty-Seven

not one to rest on my laurels

My mind is constantly thinking, that can be a curse as well as an advantage. Other than the 'Nashville Rat' I have had a couple of other inventions or ideas that 'almost' happened. You know those sports flags that people are always putting in their windows when supporting their local or college team? I developed a product that would connect to the car or truck, via the tailgate, the window, or the trunk that would have a tag that supported your favorite team with streamers or flags, and you would not lose it flying down the road or opening your window. I called it the Kar Klaw and I'm still trying to get that product to market. It is a tough business!

Other than writing this book, I also came up with a calendar. Driving around my home state of Tennessee working as a bus driver and a part-time mail carrier, I kept seeing all these unique mailboxes. I starting taking pictures of the most unusual or appealing ones. I developed a calendar that I have also been trying to market nationally.

For a few special packages I have included a small version of this calendar with this book, along with a CD of Smokey Jam music.

The Kar Klaw

Calendar

Smokey Jam CD

Conclusion

I have emotions running up and down me from reflecting back on my life. Things I haven't thought about for years. It reminds me of the song, *Broken Road*. Would I do it all over again? I'm not sure. But then I think about my family and all the interesting people I've met, what a whirlwind I've ridden.

All I know, it's been one killer ride from that little house on Mouse Creek!

Bill Passmore

Bill came by his musical ability the honest way. Here is Bill's dad
Carmel Passmore (far left) on spoons with his buddies.

A young Bill (3rd from left on front row) with his first band, The Spades.

The Dolphins (Bill is on drums)

The Big Brothers (Bill is 4th from left)

The Dolphins playing at Pig Alley. (Bill is 2nd from right on back row.)

The Dolphins pictured with Jane Mansfield. (Bill is 5th from the right)

The Fairlanes (Bill is standing in middle)

Bobbi and The Blenders

Past, Present and Future
(Bill is bottom left)

Past, Present & Future – Bill, James Moody, Pete Hambaugh, and Bob Shoemaker.

Smokey Jam in the early 1970's, from left, Dennis Treadwell, David Passmore, Pete Hambaugh, James Moody and Bill Passmore.

Smokey Jam in Huntsville, Alabama, from left, Dennis, James, Pete, Bill and David.

Smokey Jam in the early 1970's, from left, David, Bill, James and Dennis.

Smokey Jam at Fort Benning from left, Bill, David, Dennis and James.

Smokey Jam in the '80s, Bill, David and
Steve Garrett (the heart throb).

Smokey Jam keeping up with the musical styles – Dennis on
keyboards, David on guitar, Bill on drums, and James on Sax.

Four Wheel Drive – the band I played with on the road.
(Bill is 2nd from left)

Bill and his wife Christina, the Jam Sound Machine

Bill's daughter, Megan, with the Nashville Rat.

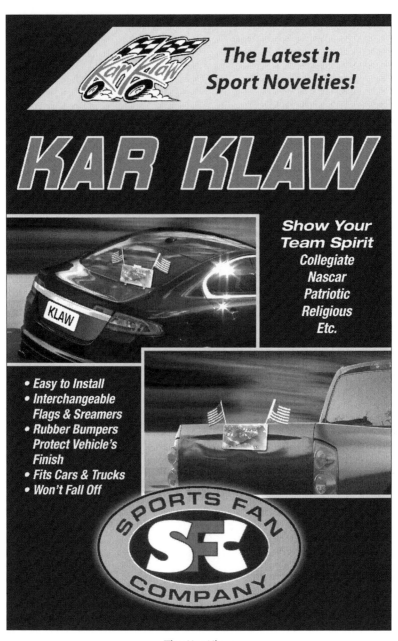

The Kar Klaw

13990912R00066

Printed in Germany
by Amazon Distribution
GmbH, Leipzig